EAST BRANCH

EAST BRANCH

Six Years on a Catskill Trout Stream

MITCH KELLER

STACKPOLE
BOOKS

Guilford, Connecticut

Published by Stackpole Books
An imprint of The Rowman & Littlefield Publishing Group, Inc.
4501 Forbes Blvd., Ste. 200
Lanham, MD 20706
www.rowman.com

Distributed by NATIONAL BOOK NETWORK

This is a work of nonfiction. The author has tried to describe experience as it actually happened, any failures or tricks of memory notwithstanding. The only made-up things in the book are the names of a few people who appear very briefly and whose privacy the author wants to protect.

British Library Cataloguing in Publication Information available

Library of Congress Cataloging-in-Publication Data:

Names: Keller, Mitchell, 1948- author.
Title: East Branch : six years on a Catskill trout stream / Mitch Keller.
Identifiers: LCCN 2020012598 (print) | LCCN 2020012599 (ebook) | ISBN 9780811739375 (hardback) | ISBN 9780811769327 (epub)
Subjects: LCSH: Keller, Mitchell, 1948- | Fishers—New York (State)—Catskill Mountains Region—Biography. | Brown trout fishing—New York (State)—Delaware River, East Branch. | Brown trout fisheries—New York (State)—Delaware River, East Branch. | Fly fishing— New York (State)—Delaware River, East Branch—Anecdotes. | Delaware River, East Branch (N.Y.)—Biography. | Catskill Mountains Region (N.Y.)—Biography.
Classification: LCC SH20.K45 A3 2020 (print) | LCC SH20.K45 (ebook) | DDC 639.2092 [B]—dc23
LC record available at https://lccn.loc.gov/2020012598
LC ebook record available at https://lccn.loc.gov/2020012599

∞™ The paper used in this publication meets the minimum requirements of American National Standard for Information Sciences—Permanence of Paper for Printed Library Materials, ANSI/ NISO Z39.48-1992.

In memory of
Mitchell and Patricia Covington Keller

Every river that flows is good, and has something worthy to be loved.

—HENRY VAN DYKE, *LITTLE RIVERS*

Contents

ACKNOWLEDGMENTS

I am grateful to Diane Galusha, author, president of the Historical Society of the Town of Middletown, and former editor of the *Catskill Mountain News*, for her careful reading of chapter 3 and the corrections and improvements I was able to make as a result.

I'd like to thank Dr. Robert Titus, paleontologist, author, and journalist, for taking the time to clarify my understanding of how the East Branch Delaware formed.

Thanks also to Chris VanMaaren, Region 4 fisheries manager for the New York State Department of Environmental Conservation, for helping me sort through the confusion over the name of the East Branch tributary (Dry Brook? Bush Kill?) in Arkville.

And a special note of gratitude to Rima Walker, of Andes, New York, for her unwavering kindness and generosity during the years I lived in the cabin.

PART ONE

THE CALL OF TROUT COUNTRY

Living in New York City in the 1980s, always poor and often broke because all I wanted to do was write, I took the Short Line bus whenever I could up to Roscoe, that tiny village in the Catskill Mountains where fly fishing is a way of life.

I'd get off at the Roscoe Diner, hoist a seedy old backpack stuffed with fishing gear onto my shoulders, and hike a mile or more to a solitary stretch of the upper Beaverkill. There I would fish intently and joyously until the bittersweet moment when I had to reel in, pack up, and hurry back to the diner for the bus home. Often I was able to fish for little more than four precious hours, but even that was worth six round-trip hours on a bus.

Sometimes I had enough money to stay overnight in one of the twenty-dollar rooms at the old Antrim Lodge in Roscoe, and after fishing till dark could be on the stream again at dawn. Occasionally I was able to rent or borrow a car and could range over the entire Catskill region, fishing not just the Beaverkill and Willowemoc Creek, which meets the Beaverkill at Roscoe, but other rivers like the Neversink, the Esopus, the Schoharie, and the East and West Branches of the Delaware. A couple of times I wandered up into the Adirondacks to fish the West Branch of the Ausable.

5

It seemed that whenever I did leave the city, it was usually to go fishing. Whatever money I did have to spend was spent on fishing. Fly fishing had also become increasingly conspicuous in the almost wholly unremunerative writing I was trying to do. Trout streams and the life within them and the places they ran reached something deep inside me that I desperately needed to reach. I loved the sport more with each passing year and wanted to be good at it. I loved the green, pastoral, soothing landscape of the Catskills, with its operatic skies, sleepy villages that seemed stuck in time, and clean rushing water everywhere. I loved New York City, too, but not so much that I couldn't do without it.

For years I'd been telling myself that one day I was going to make the break and go live full-time on a trout river, at least for a while—a year, two years, the rest of my life, who could tell? The time to act finally came when my landlord, whose indulgence and generosity had helped see me through for almost a decade, informed me that he'd sold the brownstone I lived in and that I would have to leave my ridiculously cheap apartment. Since staying in the city was financially impossible, I was free to start looking for a place to live in the Catskill trout country. I couldn't have been more excited. I was ready for this.

I began my search for a new home in Roscoe. I had already spent so much time in Roscoe over the past seven or eight years that I felt at home there. I knew the streets, the eating and drinking places, the fly shops, the faces in town, even some of the stories behind the faces. I knew the bartender at the Antrim Lodge and had spent my share of nights there. Besides, what more could an Eastern fly fisherman ask than to live on the Beaverkill? What painter wouldn't want to live next to the Metropolitan Museum, or musician next to Carnegie Hall?

But I couldn't find a place in Roscoe that I both wanted to live in and could afford. Disappointed at first, I quickly came to see this as a blessing. The Beaverkill was world-famous, its best pools and runs heavily fished; it belonged to everyone, and sometimes it seemed that everyone was there. I preferred to fish in solitude. Why not seek out water that wasn't such a gathering place?

Studying my maps of the Catskill Mountains, I decided that the village of Margaretville was worth a look. Less than an hour's drive northeast of Roscoe, Margaretville (1990 population: 639) was situated on the East Branch of the Delaware on New York State Routes 30 and 28, the latter being the main east-west highway through the central Catskills. It was a few miles upstream of the Pepacton Reservoir, which impounded the East Branch for some twenty miles before the river emerged from the dam at the village of Downsville. After Downsville, I saw on my maps, the East Branch ran southwest about twenty-five more highway miles, absorbing the Beaverkill along the way and finally merging with the West Branch Delaware to form the main Delaware River.

It's important to note here that the East Branch above the Pepacton and the East Branch below it are very different trout rivers. The upstream East Branch, the one at Margaretville, is at the mercy of seasonal variations in air temperature and rainfall; it regularly becomes too warm and low to fish, often for months at a time. The East Branch below the Pepacton, thanks to releases from the bottom of the reservoir, provides miles of cold, high-quality trout habitat all season long. When anglers other than those who live in or near Margaretville refer in casual conversation to the East Branch, they almost always mean only the tailwater, the long upper part of which has a well-deserved place among the elite Catskill trout streams. The East Branch I was considering has nowhere near the same stature and draws nowhere near the same number of fishermen, which is one of the reasons it was so attractive to me.

I did recall reading somewhere that the late A.J. McClane, one of the most accomplished anglers and angling writers of the twentieth century, had done much of his youthful fishing in and around Margaretville, though he was not a native of the region. But that was the only claim to fame for this water that I knew of. The fact is, the East Branch above the Pepacton hasn't gotten much ink in the extensive literature of Catskill fly fishing. There are reference guides that barely mention it. I immediately and very naturally started calling it the "upper" East Branch (and still do), but soon learned that many fishermen use that designation only for the seventeen miles of tailwater between Downsville and the Beaverkill confluence—after which comes the "lower" East Branch, which is not as fine a trout river. It was as if the topographic upper East Branch didn't even exist.

My maps, in the seductive way that maps can, made the part of the river running between Margaretville and the reservoir look secluded and inviting. They showed that Esopus Creek, a major rainbow-trout river, was only a short drive down Route 28 in the direction of Kingston and Woodstock. The Beaverkill, the Willowemoc, the tailwater East Branch, and the uppermost West Branch of the Delaware, little more than twenty miles to the north, were all within comfortable driving distance. Nearby, in addition to the East Branch, were a number of smaller, less-known streams, including the Bush Kill and the Tremper Kill.

In short, Margaretville seemed an excellent place for a serious fly fisherman to establish his headquarters, and on July 30, 1990, I moved into a rented cabin in the hemlock woods on a mountainside about a mile from the village.

Apart from what I had gleaned from my fishing books and maps, I knew nothing about my new town. I had never fished the East Branch above the reservoir. I had been in Margaretville only twice, both times very briefly, the last time at night while passing through on a fishing trip three or four years earlier. Leaving Route 28 and crossing the river on the Bridge Street Bridge, I drove up to Main Street just to snoop around a bit, as I always like to do in an unfamiliar town. It was summer, but Main Street was empty. The one locus of bright light and activity was the tiny Village Pub, from which there burst a din of music and voices every time someone went in or came out. The sky was clear and moonlit, and I could see the dark, soft outlines of the mountains that hugged the village on all sides, close and intimate in the Catskill fashion. I remember thinking that the setting must be very pretty when the mountains were ablaze in the fall.

That was, as I say, the second time I'd been in Margaretville. My first brief stop there preceded the second by five or six years. My then girlfriend and I were riding the Trailways bus from New York up to Delhi, the seat of Delaware County—Margaretville's county—to spend the weekend at a friend's rural retreat. We weren't getting along and weren't talking much, which left a lot of time for looking out the window.

As the bus advanced up 28, I was more and more taken with the loveliness of the country—the deep-green mountains that seemed almost close enough to touch; the classic-looking trout river that coursed and tumbled not far from the highway, skewing south as we did north. Esopus Creek. It was a cool, gloomy, misty day, big gray clouds clinging to the hills, and I imagined how pretty everything I was seeing must be in sunlight, under blue skies. Landscape can talk to us, and in this one, this verdant place of low, round, gentle mountains interlaced with so much cold running water, I recognized something of myself. I perceived it as a landscape I could be comfortable in. The fact that the Catskills were also one of the legendary regions of American fly fishing didn't hurt.

By the time the bus made its scheduled stop at the Inn Between Restaurant in Margaretville—a town I'd never heard of—I was telling myself that one day I was going to live in these parts and pursue the life of a committed angler. I *knew* it.

Now, all these years later, I was moving into a cabin from which, if I cut through the woods on the mountainside sloping down to Route 28, as I often did over the next six years, I could walk to the Inn Between in ten minutes. This nearness to the site of my epiphany often struck me as interesting, and still does, but I believe it was far more coincidental than spiritual. Margaretville simply turned out to be the place best situated for everything I wanted: a trout stream that got comparatively little fishing pressure, a base from which other rivers could easily be reached, and, just as important, affordable habitation for a fisherman and freelance writer whose total dollar resources at any given time almost never exceeded three digits, often didn't exceed two, and occasionally dipped into the singles. I should add here that I didn't have a clue how I was going to pay my bills in Margaretville.

⌁

I found the cabin after some diligent legwork and a key tip from the woman tending bar at the Village Pub. It was ridiculously close to the ideal of the private, quiet, inexpensive sylvan abode I had often imagined myself living in one day. The moment I saw it, I said to myself, *That's it, that's the place.*

The one-story cabin had brown clapboard siding and a gently pitched roof of pale-green asphalt shingles. It had been built in the 1960s, mainly for warm-weather use. To reach it, you drove half a mile up a steep, narrow, winding road off Route 28, then turned right onto a dirt road and went a few hundred yards more. The cabin was on the right, well back from the dirt road at the bottom of a grassy slope—the front yard. Behind it were woods. Unkempt litters of hemlock and birch bordered the yard on each side and shielded the one-acre site from similar dwellings, only sporadically occupied, on the adjacent properties. There were many raspberry bushes and one apple tree. The big picture window in the kitchen, flanked by two smaller windows and then yellowish-cream shutters, looked out on the front yard and upward to the looming side of a forested mountain, Pakatakan by name, and the sky above it. Thousands of acres of state land, right across the road.

To the left of the cabin as you approached it coming down through the yard was a wooden storage shed. When I moved in, I was ignorant enough to store a cardboard box containing ancient personal papers in this shed, only to discover years later that creatures had feasted on my college blue-book exams. To the right of the cabin and a little behind it was another shed, made of metal and painted the same brown as the cabin. Attached to its side was a huge, clocklike U-Haul thermometer stuck on sixty-two.

Off the left side of the cabin was a nice little deck made of treated lumber. To enter the cabin, you stepped onto the deck and went through a screen door into a narrow, screened porch whose floor tilted several degrees down and away from the cabin. The roof over the porch was gently peaked and had a scalloped decorative trim, slightly tacky, that matched the kitchen shutters in color.

The front door opened from the porch into the living room. To the right of the living room was the kitchen. Behind the living room were two very small bedrooms and a tiny bathroom. That was the extent of the place, which had a very distinct odor that I still remember fondly, a blend of mustiness and wood with a dash of propane.

All the walls were covered with cheap fake-wood paneling. The living room floor was covered wall to wall with all-weather carpeting, dark red. Underneath the carpeting was plywood, and not far below the plywood was the ground. Here and there in corners of the living room and the other rooms were inhabited spiderwebs.

The cabin was furnished, a big plus since I had very little furniture of my own. In the living room were two vinyl armchairs, one emerald green and starting to crack, little bits of stuffing emerging from the fissures; the other a creamy white with broad, useful wooden armrests and, embossed on the backrest, a big head of a smiling horse. Also, a musty couch-bed; a cheap coffee table; a pair of junky, hideous floor lamps; a small bookcase; and a couple of wall cabinets. An old propane heater, as big as a small chest of drawers and sturdy enough to sit on as the heat was coming up on cold mornings, undoubtedly original with the cabin, was tucked into a corner.

Not counting the funny horse chair, which was very comfortable, the best feature of the living room was the fine raised-hearth fireplace, which was going to get more use over the next six winters than probably any other fireplace in the Catskill Mountains.

The bedrooms had linoleum floors, but the linoleum had detached in places from the surface underneath and become wavy with air pockets. On the walls of each bedroom were two or three dime-store pictures of outdoor scenes, which I never touched. I had my own bed to put in one of the rooms; the other came with two folding beds and a bureau. My bedroom had the cabin's only closet, on the shelves of which were some old bed linens, neatly folded and stacked but mildewy. I left them that way for the duration.

As for the cramped little bathroom, the overwhelming impression there was one of plumbing, of tanks, valves, hoses, and copper pipes everywhere. In addition to the toilet, the small sink (rubber stopper on chain), and the white metal shower stall, which was somewhat warped and rusted, the cabin's propane water heater was there and took up much of the space. The pipe carrying water from the well entered the cabin under the sink and spawned a network of hoses and copper pipes going to the sink, the toilet, the shower, the water heater, and on through the wall into the kitchen. The water heater spawned a separate copper network of its own. In the coming winters I would learn all about copper water pipes and would get good at fixing them when they burst.

The kitchen, almost as big as the living room, was the brightest space in the house because of its large, unobstructed picture window. The floor was linoleum, a red-brick pattern, in spots buckled and wavy. Next to the window was a cool diner-style table with three chairs that matched it and one that didn't. There were a four-burner gas stove, a black rotary wall phone, a Philco refrigerator that looked right out of the 1940s, and an electric clock of similar vintage on the wall above the Philco.

All things considered, it was a splendid place to live. Sitting on the screened porch those first few evenings, watching deer, raccoons, skunks, rabbits, woodchucks, and turkeys wander through the yard, listening to the crickets, feeling the luxurious soothing silence in my skull, watching the moon climb up from behind Pakatakan Mountain and floodlight the sky, I think I was as happy as I'd ever been. Finally I had space. Finally I had silence. Finally I lived in a place where I could be on a trout stream any day I wanted, with the fly rod leaning against the wall, the vest and waders hanging nearby, the river just minutes away. Finally I had made it happen.

It was the silence that affected me the most. For the past nine and a half years, I had lived in a ground-floor, street-front studio apartment on the Upper West Side of Manhattan. Sometimes, especially when the windows were wide open, it was like living on a traffic island in a busy intersection: engines, horns, the grinding of garbage trucks, police sirens, fire sirens, ambulance sirens, three noisy shift changes at the nursing home next door, conversations, arguments, the verbal violence of road rage, passing boom boxes (no iPods or smartphones in those days), homeless people going noisily through the garbage cans at all hours, occasionally the screams and shouts of people who'd just been mugged or in some other way scared silly, a couple of times the running feet of a mugger; even, once or twice, not that far away, gunshots. What was remarkable was how easily I adjusted to it all. After a certain early point, I hardly even heard it. I even slept through it. It just became part of my dreams.

Those were the years of the crack epidemic, of prowling desperado crackheads. One night I came home to find that my apartment had been broken into, a complete waste of time and effort for the criminal since I owned nothing of the slightest worth to him. Another time, in the middle of the afternoon while I was out, a neighbor surprised a young man who was trying to bash in my apartment door with a concrete block. The young man fled but left me with one nasty-looking door. Late one night I had to call the police when I heard shrieks for help coming from the brownstone next door. The man shrieking was being stabbed by the guy who lived in the adjacent apartment; apparently they'd hated and baited each other for years. And I mustn't forget the truly insane-sounding group meetings of some sort, with screaming, wailing, sustained foot-stomping, and loud applause, that took place for a while in the apartment upstairs.

So when I made the abrupt switch to my mountainside cabin, the pervasive silence was a revelation. It was like a balm inside my ears, a long, slow, deep massage of my needful brain.

Having no television, and getting only a couple of regional stations on the radio, I started listening at nights on the shortwave bands, getting my news and entertainment from London, Tokyo, Moscow, Beijing, and Utah. The voices crackling in through the night from these faraway places, telling me about the start of the first Gulf War—Iraq had just invaded Kuwait—agricultural practices in provincial Russia, and cricket scores in India, seemed only to intensify my newfound silence and solitude. So did the lonesome-sounding drumming on the roof of the rain that fell so hard and so often, usually for long, unbroken hours at a time, during my first two weeks in the cabin.

As the rain allowed, I began exploring the upper East Branch and its surroundings. I came to the river knowing little more about it than what I'd learned from looking at it on maps and out a car window. Spending time hiking up and down its banks, acquainting myself with both the obvious and not-so-obvious access points, was a good start. I was able to cover much of the river from where it passes through town to where the reservoir begins, getting trapped in the woods a few times during rainstorms; getting lost in them in the dark; gradually learning my way around that green, lush, gnarly, buggy, fragrant world.

I fished, too, of course, though not very well or successfully. My first decent trout, a well-fed brown of twelve inches, came only after I had repeatedly caught nothing but small stockies and chubs or been skunked. One thing that surprised and delighted me was that I rarely saw another angler, and when I did, he was always the *only* one. This river certainly seemed to bear out the old chestnut that ninety percent of the fishermen fish ten percent of the water.

Unfortunately, although two months remained in the East Branch season when I moved to Margaretville, I was able to take only partial advantage of them. My hopes of settling into the sweet life of a full-time trout man soon came up against a familiar obstacle: financial reality, the governing reality of our lives. I was broke again; the move upstate had wiped me out. I was not the free man I'd been pretending to be; no one who needs money is. My fishing would have to be set aside so that I could make enough dough to pay some bills and get through the next few months.

And so, barely a month after moving in, I was doing what so many native Catskillians have always had to do: going elsewhere to earn money. For the past six or seven years, I had survived mainly by working as a sort of freelance, all-purpose laborer on renovation projects in New York City. This allowed me to get my writing done free of the mind drain of mentally demanding employment, and my fishing done in the often large blocks of time between jobs. Now I was going to seek the help of my friends in the city one last time. After that I would somehow have to make my money locally.

The sense of financial urgency was heightened one morning in the third week of August when I was looking out my big kitchen window and watching the morning cloud cover break up on the great green wall of Pakatakan Mountain. Suddenly I saw something I hadn't seen before. It was a small splash of yellow high up on the mountain, a single yellow patch in all the green. It looked as if a giant had cracked an egg over one of the trees and let the yolk spill all over it. Hardly had I moved into my cabin, and already the first sign of the coming winter—the first changing tree—had appeared. Already the hawk had taken wing and was slowly on its way. Catskill winters are very cold, gray, snowy, and long. All the more reason, for a little while, at least, to put the building up of my resources ahead of my fishing.

CHAPTER TWO

Earlier times—A fisherman's progress—
First fly rod—The big bang—Stranded in
the city—Escape to the Beaverkill—
Jim Deren—The trusty Adams—Roscoe
and the Antrim—A wandering angler

I HAD NO TEACHER OR MENTOR IN FISHING, EITHER IN OR OUTSIDE my family, and had to come to it by myself. I'm sure my father never held a fishing rod in his hands in all his adult life. Although he never said so, it wouldn't have surprised me to learn that, like many people, he considered all fishing boring, an activity engaged in by whooping, beer-swilling yahoos, underoccupied old men getting away from their wives, and the innately dull.

After I became a fly fisherman, I tried once or twice to explain to him that fly fishing was far more interesting and challenging than other methods, and that serious people could and did devote their lives to understanding its complexities and pursuing its beauties. But none of it meant anything to him, and I suspect he still thought that when his eldest son went fishing, he impaled some small living thing on a hook, tossed it into the water, sat down on the bank, and waited, perhaps reading a magazine or taking a nap in the process. I've wondered if he had moments of pensive reflection on this curious, vaguely disappointing part of his son's makeup.

He did, on one important occasion, grandly indulge my youthful interest in fishing. For our family vacation one summer when I was ten or eleven, he drove us from our suburban Connecticut home all the way up to Moosehead Lake in Maine, by far the greatest distance we had ever traveled. It was an unforgettable experience for me. I had the use of a rowboat and would go out in it alone and dangle my baited line in the gloriously clear, sun-filled water, watching the colorful perch and sunfish peck at my offering and sometimes get hooked. We stayed in a simple cabin in which the electricity went off at a set time every night, leaving us in darkness, with nothing to do but go to sleep. Since such a place was so totally not my father, whose idea of the outdoors was a casual round of golf or an easygoing day of skiing, or a comfortable lawn chair and a book, I had sometimes wondered as an adult why he took us way the hell up to wild Moosehead Lake. I asked him this when he was in his eighties, and his immediate reply was, "You wanted to go fishing."

We lived in a beach town on Long Island Sound, not far from New York City, to which many of the men (though not my father) commuted to work. It was a boating town; a sailing town; a seafood, clamming, foghorn-at-night town. As a boy, I spent a lot of time at the beach, fished from a bridge for snappers—juvenile bluefish—and even for a while had my own fourteen-foot runabout.

But I never had a great natural love for the salt. It was just there. I preferred the woods, which began where our little backyard ended. The woods were mysterious and exciting and strangely comforting. I liked all their silent solitary places where I could be alone, invisible, unfindable. Since then, the woods I wandered and poked around in as a child have been almost entirely consumed by subdivisions, but at that time they were extensive enough to allow me to imagine what the place I lived in must have been like before the white man came. I'd sit on a big rock and think, *An Indian my age must have sat on this same rock hundreds of years ago.* I'd hear a car go down the quiet, shaded blacktop fifty yards through the trees—Witch Lane, it was called—and feel that the car and the people in it belonged to a completely different world from the one I was in at that moment, a world I would shortly have to return to but could leave again simply by walking into the woods.

Similarly, it was the water in the woods that interested me the most, in particular a brook that ran not far behind our house whose name, if it had one, I never knew. In places its channel was not more than three or four feet wide. It followed a long, fairly straight course before finally making a big turn and then running downhill through the woods to sea level, where it flattened out and welled up in a marsh next to an inlet of the Sound. I never saw a single fish in that brook, but I wasn't looking for any. I just liked being there, hearing the water trickle over the stones, looking into the bottom pockets of sand and gravel that gleamed and trembled in the sun, smelling the mud when the water was low. It seems to me now that I perceived that little stream as very much a world unto itself, separate, ancient, unfathomable in origin, source of much of the surrounding life, mute witness to unknowable history, thrillingly apart from and indifferent to the world I came from and lived in. The Sound, with its vast openness reaching to the hazy horizon, its hundreds of boats, its throbbing engines, its crowded beaches and picnic areas, its laughing, shouting swimmers, its little airplanes dragging commercial messages across the sky, did not compare for me with the mystery and allure of that humble, nameless brook in the woods. Nor, needless to say, was it as good a place to be by myself. We are who we are very early in life.

In those days, and for many years to come, I didn't even know there was such a thing as fly fishing. There was no one to tell me about it. Maybe I would have learned about it if I'd had some exposure to the outdoor magazines, but I didn't, even at the barbershop. If I had started coming home with magazines whose covers showed guys in camo holding rifles and posing with dead animals, my parents wouldn't have known what to make of it. They would have quietly discussed it while I was in the next room watching TV. In our world, the hook-and-bullet magazines like *Field & Stream* and *Outdoor Life* were about as likely to be seen on the coffee table as *Wrestling Confidential* and *True Detective*. That was a very long time before the movie version of *A River Runs through It* and the fly-fishing vogue it caused, when everybody seemed to know about fly fishing and half of them were going to fly shops to gear up.

So, unlike many fly fishers today, I was not able to cut straight to the highest form of fishing. I had to find my way there by going through all the unsexy lower forms first. As a young boy, I fished ponds for sunfish and the edges of the Sound for whatever would bite, using hand lines, sinkers, hardware-store rods, rusty bait-casting reels, bobbers, worms, shiners, and bread balls. Even into my mid-twenties I was contentedly casting heavy sinkers from shore to deliver sandworms to flounder, and using chunks of bunker to catch bluefish. Eventually I more or less abandoned saltwater fishing in favor of spin fishing for largemouth and smallmouth bass in ponds, lakes, and streams, using Mepps lures, Rooster Tails, Rapala broken-backs, and Dardevle Spoons. In addition to the bass, I caught plenty of down-market fish like bluegills, perch, and pickerel, and was glad to have them.

Not that I was fishing much in those years anyway. I had become a young newspaperman and was happily immersed in the work and the life. Stories, writing, reporting, reading, talking, thinking, ideas, girlfriends, booze, pot, partying, hanging out, and all the joys, disappointments, and trials of young adulthood and city life took over. I hardly gave fishing a thought. For all I knew, it would remain only an occasional pastime for the rest of my life. I believe I was all right with that, too, though, as I say, I just didn't think about it.

Then came a time of gnawing unhappiness when my heart and soul were ailing and my legs, as they dutifully hauled me from one gray day to the next, felt as if they'd been filled with mud. Having already learned that lots of alcohol and relentless work were not the answer—though the effectiveness of work in helping to cure unhappiness is real—it was fishing I turned to for solace and restoration, a ladder out of the gloom. This seemed to be instinctive, a reversion to the comfort, the haven, of fundamental personal things. I found a little stream and a couple of ponds in the cranberry country of southeastern Massachusetts, in Plymouth County, and across the bridge in Barnstable County on Cape Cod, and my trips from Boston down to these sanctuaries on weekends and days off were what I lived for. It is no exaggeration to say that fishing saw me through.

That was when I started thinking more and more about fly fishing. Of course, by then I had long known about this higher level of the sport, one that had its own tackle, language, and culture and seemed both more refined and more demanding than the fishing I'd always done. My awareness of fly fishing had grown very gradually over the years, mainly, I think, from reading the "Outdoors" columns in the *New York Times* by the always engaging Nelson Bryant. I'm quite sure that those columns, and perhaps a few by the great sportswriter Red Smith, who loved fly fishing and also wrote for the *Times*, were my first exposure to the sport's mystique and lovely vocabulary, which for all its charms was difficult to comprehend.

Now, though, I knew I had to take the big step and actually become a fly fisherman. I was still playing checkers; I had to advance to chess. I don't think it was any one thing that prompted this change in my fishing consciousness. Certainly it wasn't a person—I still didn't know any fly fishermen, and had never, so far as I knew, even met one. There wasn't a fly fisherman, even just a dilettante fly fisherman, in every other house in those days, as there often seems to be now. Maybe it was simply that, since I was now doing so much more fishing, I was also reading more in the outdoor magazines, trying to get bass tips from writers like Homer Circle in *Sports Afield* (which still covered fishing then), and as a consequence the fly-fishing content in the magazines was seeping osmotically into my mind, pushing my curiosity to the tipping point. I suspect it was something like that.

At any rate, on Saturday, May 5, 1979, I drove to the Orvis Shop of Boston, which despite its name was in suburban Wayland, Massachusetts, and told the sales clerk I wanted to get started in fly fishing. The receipt from that day, which I still have (just in case I have to bring something back), shows that for $33.95 I bought a "Cortland WF5F outfit." That confuses me now, because while it definitely was an outfit—everything came in one big box—the rod, a seven-and-a-half-foot Cortland Pro-Crest, which I still have, has Recommended for Line 6/7 written on it, and I'm pretty sure I did use it with a six-weight. Since I didn't know anything about line weights at the time and was completely at the mercy of the sales clerk, I don't know if he simply made a mistake writing "WF5F" on the receipt or if I did in fact end up with the wrong line for the rod. All I do know is that my Cortland Pro-Crest, once my inexperienced hands finally started casting it, felt just fine.

The rod was fiberglass, two pieces, light brown with reddish-brown wrappings; the line, to the best of my memory, a "rocket" taper, in color kind of beige or tan. Also in the box were a dark red Cortland reel, a couple of tapered leaders, and an instructional booklet. For $17.95 I bought a separate, prepackaged "fly selection" of fifteen flies; the patterns included Adams, March Brown, Quill Gordon, Hendrickson, Light Cahill, Hare's Ear, Muddler Minnow, Black-Nosed Dace, and Black Ant. The receipt also shows that I bought an Orvis spinning reel and had it mounted with six-pound-test line, an indication that I was still holding back from an all-out conversion to fly fishing.

Indeed, for the rest of that year and into the next, that box stood against the wall in a corner of my apartment, unopened. I don't think

I even cracked its seal. I remember it so well. Sometimes I'd just sit and stare at it. I suspect I felt a little anxious about it, knowing as I did that it meant I was going to have to learn about fishing all over again, start acquiring a whole new body of knowledge. Perhaps I also intuited that once I started casting that rod, if only on the grass, I would be a goner.

Finally, a month or so before the start of another fishing season, I assembled the parts of my "outfit," went to the park across the street, and started teaching myself to fly cast. For better or worse, no doubt often worse, I am an autodidact in all things in which I can get away with being an autodidact. My main instruction came from an excellent "fly fishing handbook" I had bought, published by Scientific Anglers. But I loved casting that supersoft rod from the start—fly casting can be addictive all by itself, even just on grass—and practiced regularly in preparation for the big day, the day I would become a fly fisherman.

The day came. I drove from Boston down to the small stream in Plymouth County where I'd been spending so much time. It was the outflow of Little Herring Pond, feeding Great Herring Pond, and I liked it mainly because I always had it entirely to myself, but also because it was loaded with smallmouth bass and had a few large-mouths, too, as well as many pickerel that seemed to me particularly fierce and ravenous. Once on this stream I had launched a long down-stream cast of a Dardevle Spoon only to see the line come down on a high branch of a tree, the spoon then plunging at great speed straight down into the water. I immediately tried to pull the cast back, but as I yanked the spoon as hard as I could up out of the water, hoping to clear the branch with it and get it back, a pickerel was already attached to it, and the pickerel ended up stuck on the branch way up in the tree. The only way I could save it from what surely would have been a hideous and humiliating death for a fish—hanging in a tree! being pecked to the bones by birds!—was to cut the line and hope the pickerel fell back into the stream. Which it did, albeit with the lure, trailing fifty or sixty feet of monofilament, still in its mouth.

I found a wide-open space on the bank where I could cast without having to worry about trees. For my first fly I chose, naturally enough, a dry, the type of fly most identified with fly fishing. I'm not positive, all these years later, but I believe it was a March Brown. I seem to recall thinking that in name and appearance, the March Brown suited the landscape of that early-spring day in New England, and as a rank beginner, I was looking for whatever connections I could make. In actuality, of course, the mayfly imitated by the March Brown pattern, *Maccaffertium vicarium*, appears on Eastern rivers in May and June. But I didn't know this yet. I didn't really know much of anything.

Attaching the fly to my leader tippet with a Duncan loop, I cast it from the bank into the slow-moving stream. I don't think I expected anything to happen, still not quite believing, perhaps, that hungry fish would be interested in that weightless little clump of feather and fur way up there on the surface. So when a fish suddenly rose from the depths and took a vigorous swipe at the fly—a rejection, or maybe a miss, but a slashing, aggressive one—I was stunned. At that very moment I went through a major brain-cell reorganization. It was a new neurological order, completed in less than a second, like the big bang.

I don't remember if I caught a fish that day. I probably didn't, but it hardly mattered. All at once the spinners, spoons, and plugs in my tackle box looked crude and archaic. Even the tackle box itself— heavy-duty plastic, two-tone brown—looked *done*. It is an old story in fishing. From that day forward there would be no more hardware; no more treble hooks; no more metal and plastic and paint; no more gaudy gizmos that fluttered, wobbled, wriggled, and whirled. There would be only flies.

In that first season of my fly-fishing life, the places I fished and the fish I fished for didn't change much. I still sought mostly largemouth and smallmouth bass, both of which were always willing to smash my imperfectly presented flies. It would be a good while yet before I went up against a fastidiously selective brown trout. I did go looking for trout a couple of times in the adjoining Mashpee and Wakeby Ponds on Cape Cod, and I'm sure I saw a few hugging the bottom as I waded around in my hip waders. But they ignored my surface flies, and I didn't yet know how to go after them down deep.

The first real trout fishing I ever did was late that summer when I went to Warner, New Hampshire, to do a little angling with my old college friend Pete, who lived there. Pete excelled at catching lunker largemouths with artificial worms; he had the touch. He and I had fished for largemouths a few times in Bagley Pond, an excellent bass pond not far from his house, but this time we also went to the Warner River for brook trout. I cast my dry flies upstream, just as all the books and magazine articles I'd been reading said to do, and the little brookies came up and took them. It was about as elementary as dry-fly fishing for trout gets. But it was a start, and it made me indescribably happy. I was a real fly fisherman now, a trout man.

I still hadn't learned about catch and release, though. The brookies were delicious.

I also went that trip to the Contoocook River in Henniker, New Hampshire, but it was very fast and turbulent my one day there and I had no idea how to fish such water with flies. Call it my first skunking.

For some reason I was still bringing my old tackle box and all of its obsolete contents with me every time I went fishing. I guess I thought that something in the box might eventually come in handy. One evening I had waded perhaps fifty feet out into Little Herring Pond, which is very shallow, and was casting a Hornberg. Glancing behind me, I saw another fisherman walking through the spot where I'd put the tackle box, apparently leaving for the night. I hadn't even known he was around. When I looked that way again a few minutes later, my box was gone.

I hurried out of the water and up through the woods to the little parking area. My car was the only one there. Still in my waders, I climbed in and set out to catch the thief, my fully assembled Cortland Pro-Crest sticking out the window. I had a fast, wonderful car, a 1970 Chevy Malibu, V-8, 350 cubic inches, dark green, and I hated having to beat it up by racing along the potholed, deeply rutted dirt roads leading back to the highways. But I was enraged and thought I had a good chance of catching the SOB. He must have flown out of there, though, because I didn't see another car anywhere along those back roads, and I looked all over. To steal a man's tackle box when his back is turned—well, it pleases me to know that anyone who'd do that has probably had a crappy life anyway.

My rebirth as a fly fisherman coincided with the start of many years of financial hardship that I accepted as the cost of a proper bohemian life. To this day I consider the dreary arts of living without money to be one of my few areas of expertise. If the economic cataclysm that I've heard the crackpot seers of late-night talk radio predict from time to time really does come, leaving the country in ruins, I'll do just fine.

Not long after that first season of fly fishing, I was back in New York, my home city if not my hometown. I had left my newspaper job and was hoping to survive solely on the spawn of my electric type-writer. This was, of course, a nearly impossible aspiration, as droves of former "freelance writers" over the generations, including no small number in the outdoor fields like fishing and hunting, would attest. But I was young and tireless and undaunted and gave it my best shot, sitting there at my little card table day after day, month after month, wearing out my Smith Corona. It's actually a bit of a stretch to say I was a freelance writer because that implies a certain practical, calculated, businesslike effort to secure contracts for writing before doing the writing, whereas I just wrote what I wanted to write, the way I wanted to write it, and then tried to sell the finished product. Good luck with that!

Predictably, before long all my money was gone—even the Chevy Malibu had been sold—and, with the occasional, invaluable help of a pawnshop on Broadway, I was living on soybeans, sardines, and Kraft macaroni, but mostly on coffee and cigarettes. Cigarettes were cheap then. For some unfathomable reason, I just couldn't get *Harper's*, *The Atlantic Monthly*, and *The New Yorker*, among other publications, to pay me for the essays and stories I sent them. Even a long piece I wrote on how to teach yourself fly fishing ("The most important decision you must make at the outset is that you will not be intimidated") was turned down by *Sports Afield*—though, I must say, very graciously—as "too basic" for its readership. That rejection was particularly hard to take—I still remember the bitter sting of reading the letter, the wave of despondency—because I had really believed they were going to accept the article, and by then things had become dire. I'd spent my last nine cents on three pretzel sticks in a bodega on Columbus Avenue. I was using coffee grounds and tea bags a second time, and was making my own smokes with rolling paper and recycled tobacco from ashtray butts. Even the professional panhandlers up on Broadway had started to pick up the vibe, and hardly bothered with me anymore.

I had been chronically penniless once before, as a very young man scrounging my way around Europe for a year, so I'd had some experience at this sort of life. But in your early twenties, even being down and out can be an adventure, just a temporary inconvenience before the vast, interminable future has even begun. By your early thirties there are risks and consequences, some sort of cost, attached to just about every decision you make. Being broke at that age begins very quickly to make you not just undesirable in the larger world, but invisible. You see the process—your own disappearance—happening in people's eyes when they look at you.

Needless to say, this mean, meager life did not allow for much fly fishing, which was a constant heartache. It would have done me so much good. I thought about it and read about it all the time, and held forth on it whenever I had a willing ear. I practiced casting in the living room with the butt end of my Cortland Pro-Crest and an imaginary line. Rivers appeared frequently in my dreams; not fishing, interestingly enough, but rivers, which perhaps says something about primacy. Often these dream rivers ran through arid, barren, forbidding landscapes, sometimes at the bottom of deep canyons where they were hard to reach. Clearly, the way I was living, I had cut myself off from something of crucial importance.

Except for a few precious outings, though, I just didn't have the money, the liberty, to go fishing. I was stranded in the city, a castaway on my noisy little traffic island on the Upper West Side.

Only when I reluctantly bowed to financial reality and took a part-time job on a newspaper copy desk—the first of much part-time or temporary or irregular work I would have for years to come, almost all of it manual and a lot of it menial—was I able to resume my angling. This I did with renewed commitment. I started going up to the Catskills as often as I could, taking the subway down to the Port Authority Bus Terminal, backpack and aluminum rod tube in tow, and catching the Short Line bus for the three-hour ride to Roscoe. I don't know how many times I made this trip over the next seven or eight years, but it was many, many. Whenever I had a little time and enough money for the round-trip fare and a burger at the Roscoe Diner or a few slices of pizza at Raimondo's restaurant, I went.

Usually I took the eight a.m. bus. On the subway downtown there were always well-groomed men of my own age and background commuting to big jobs in Midtown or on Wall Street. We looked at each other as the deafening, full-tilt express train shook and swayed, perhaps seeing visions of other selves. I wanted their money and health insurance; they wanted my backpack and fishing rod. Later that day, depending mostly on the time of year and the hour when it got too dark to fish, I took either an early-evening or a late-night bus back to the city. A couple of times, in summer, I went up to Roscoe on a late-night bus and, wrapping myself in my rain poncho, tried to get a few hours' chilly sleep next to the stream so I could be on the water at dawn.

When I got off the bus at the diner, I almost always went straight to the same stretch of the upper Beaverkill, well upstream of the famous Junction Pool, where the Beaverkill merges with the Wil-lowemoc and becomes the so-called "big river"—the Beaverkill whose pools and hatches are on bucket lists of fly fishermen everywhere. The public water upstream of Junction Pool is smaller and not much fished by Beaverkill anglers. But I loved it because, in addition to having more than enough trout and trout bugs to keep me happy, it was very pretty and quiet and, especially on weekdays, I almost always had it all to myself.

I started fishing there entirely by accident. The first time I stepped off a Short Line bus in Roscoe, I had no idea where to go. I didn't know where the river was and apparently was too proud to ask. (Yes, that same phenomenon known to exasperated wives and girlfriends all over the land.) I guess I reckoned that a man should be able to sniff out a major trout river in a tiny town easily enough. So I started walking along New York State Route 206 out of the village, heading north toward Rockland, the next little commercial hub—exactly the wrong way to go to find the main Beaverkill. But I could see that the broad expanse of farmed land to my left, extending as far as I could see up

Route 206, was basically a plain bordered on my side by the road and on the far side by an abrupt rise of mountain, and I guessed there was running water where plain and mountain met. Sure enough, soon I came to a brown-and-yellow New York State fishing-access sign that directed me to the minor part of the Beaverkill that would become a major part of my fly-fishing life.

That humble stretch of the Beaverkill—I fished it for probably a mile or so upstream of the access point—became both my spiritual sanctuary from the city and my fly-fishing classroom. There I intensified my course of earnest self-instruction. Few things could keep me away. If I had a chance to go upstate but it was raining, usually I went anyway; getting soaked did not count as a deterrent in those days. Sometimes, if I was hopelessly short of sleep when I got there, I'd lie down on the stones next to the stream and conk out for an hour or two. Then, waking up refreshed to the sounds of the rushing water and the breeze in the trees, all I had to do was stand up and start casting. It was more like the continuation of a dream than a normal waking up. On all those days out there alone on my sanctuary water of the Beaverkill, I had the fine feeling I was one dimension removed from the so-called real world—much like the boy in the woods I had once been. I think this sense of remove must be common among solitary anglers in trout streams.

At home I called the daily telephone recording about river and fishing conditions made by Walt Dette, the renowned Catskill fly tier, almost every morning, whether I was going fishing or not. It helped maintain my connection with the river, and there was often something to be learned from what Walt said about water temperatures and insect hatches.

And I read and reread, slowly and needfully, as if I were drawing from it nothing less than blood, oxygen, and sunlight, the great book *Trout*, by Ray Bergman, which had first come out more than forty years earlier but had aged as only the best things do: handsomely, with no loss of quality, character, or worth. It was, of course, in many respects very dated: Bergman writes at times about steel rods, silk-gut lines, and gasoline-based fly floatant. And while he is first and foremost a supremely committed fly fisherman, he gives a lot of space to spin fishing. But getting up late in the morning with a headache from long hours of reading news copy on a computer screen and opening Bergman's book was like being sprung from a windowless cell into the sunshine and fresh air, the wind, the smells of water and balsam trees. I was awed by the vastness of his knowledge and experience and by the acuity of his observations, and marked passages like the following with underlines, stars, and exclamation points:

> *Remember that on gray days there is no area where the fly is indistinct, and that this applies to any day when the sun does not cast a clearly defined shadow. On bright days, even under the shadow of the trees, the water may catch the reflection from a rock or cliff or the leaves of trees on which the sun is shining brightly, and so obscure the vision of the fish when a fly floats by in that area affected by the reflection.*
>
> *All these things must be taken into consideration when choosing the most advantageous position to fish from, and the combinations you run into are many and complicated. In fact the subject is so big that it would take a lifetime of experimentation on this idea alone to definitely arrive at some perfect conclusions.*

I was a bare-bones, fairly ragged-looking fly fisherman when I started going to the Beaverkill, prowling the stream in my cheap hip waders with my thirty-four-dollar Cortland rod and reel. I wasn't catching many decent fish yet, mostly small, stocked brown trout. I kept my flies in a plastic box jammed into a back pocket—it would be a while before I had a vest—and trimmed my monofilament with my front teeth. My flies were old, tried-and-true patterns like the Adams, Light Cahill, Royal Wulff, Royal Coachman, Leadwing Coachman, Hornberg, and Hare's Ear. I liked Muddler Minnows, but generally in smaller sizes so that I could fish them dry or wet on a light tippet. It wasn't unusual for me to have some colorful antique pattern like a McGinty or a Mickey Finn on the end of my line. I don't think many anglers use those flies anymore.

A lot of fly fishermen who lived in New York City into the early 1980s have a story about the late Jim Deren, proprietor of the late Angler's Roost fly shop in Manhattan, and I'm no different. It was Deren, who died in 1983, who got me to retire the Cortland.

One sweltering summer day I brought the butt section of the rod to his shop because its line guide had broken and I was hoping Deren would help me get it fixed. I'd been to the Angler's Roost several times before—this was the shop's third and last location, on East Forty-fourth Street near Grand Central Terminal—and always felt extremely self-conscious there. Not only could Deren be gruff, but he was very well known in the fly-fishing world and I ascribed to him comprehensive knowledge of every thing and every person associated with angling. His shop was tiny—it couldn't have been any tinier, really—and fabulously overstuffed, floor to ceiling, wall to wall, with fly-fishing merchandise and other outdoor paraphernalia. Whenever I was the only customer there, it was like being alone with Deren in a closet. As I poked around, he sat silently behind his little counter in a window that allowed a glimpse of a mysterious back room, regarding me through the lenses of his black-framed, heavy-looking glasses and the smoke of his True cigarette as he might some pathetic, clueless New York character out on the street. A couple of times he was short with me, but he seemed to soften up once he saw how sincerely I wanted to know what he did.

I handed him the butt section. He considered it a long time before saying anything, as if he were looking at something in an exhibit of Mesopotamian fishing tackle at the Museum of Natural History.

"Why don't you just get a new one?" he said, raising a possibility that hadn't occurred to me.

"I don't know," I said. "I'm happy with this one. Money's kind of tight."

Recognizing a chance to do a little business when he saw one, but also, I like to think, wanting to help bring me along as a fisherman, Deren promptly showed me two fiberglass rods within reach of where he was sitting. Each was fully assembled, as I recall, not packaged or tagged in any way. Each cost well under a hundred dollars. One was nine feet long and black, the other seven and a half feet and brown with wrappings the color of caramel. Both were five-weights. Deren encouraged me to get the nine-footer, saying it would be more versatile, but I took an immediate liking to the shorter rod and decided to buy it. I think it cost sixty-five bucks. I don't believe there was a manufacturer's name on it—I'm sure I'd remember it if there was. I also bought a new reel—I forget what make, but you can be sure it wasn't expensive—and a new five-weight line. Deren and I did well by each other that afternoon.

Unfortunately, I was able to enjoy that fine little rod for only a couple of seasons. On one Beaverkill trip when I had a car, I left the rod leaning against a fence when I drove out of the anglers' parking area after a morning's fishing. Twenty minutes later I realized what I'd done and went racing back, but the rod was gone, and all my efforts to find it failed.

Some people become attached to their possessions; some don't. I do. I coped with this upsetting experience by buying, as soon as I could, another seven-and-a-half-foot fiberglass rod that was as similar to the lost one in action and appearance as I could find. I guess I felt that if

I could duplicate the lost rod, I could lessen the sting of having lost it and help myself forget my moment of carelessness and destruction. I found my new rod—rather, my reincarnation of my lost rod—in a shop on Long Island. Both Deren and the Angler's Roost were gone by then. It was a Fisher, and it would be my main rod for many years to come.

—◦—

Of course, much of my fly-fishing preoccupation at that time was with learning about the aquatic insects that trout eat and how to imitate them with artificials. "It takes twenty years before you learn about the insects," a fisherman told me, ever so inspiringly, one night at the Antrim Lodge bar. Thank you, sir!

I remember feeling wonder, at the very beginning of my fly-fishing life, that anyone could actually be fluent in the vast, beautiful new language of trout flies that I was just starting to learn. Surely it would take decades to be able to identify all the hundreds of different patterns, with their often subtle variations in color and form and their peculiar, fanciful, highly evocative names. Looking at the color plates in my fishing books, I would despair at ever being able to tell the difference—with one quick, self-assured glance—between a Golden Duke and a Golden Ibis, a Wickham's Fancy and a Perkin's Pet, a Parmachene Belle and a Parmachene Beau. Whew! They were smart guys, these fly fishermen, with far better memories than mine. I was going to be humiliated every time I walked into a fly shop.

I learned soon enough, of course, that I didn't need to know all those multitudinous patterns; did not, in fact, need to know more than a tiny fraction of them. I learned that there were almost as many theories about trout flies as there were trout fishermen, and that while some fishermen liked to arm themselves with many hundreds of flies, others preferred to carry an all-purpose few. One Beaverkill angler, dismissing the use of any other flies as unnecessary, boasted to me

36

that he used only two patterns, March Browns and Black Ants, all year long. I didn't want to become quite that eccentric, but it was clear early on that I tended toward the reductive point of view, my natural bent doubtless reinforced by those continually recycled articles in the hook-and-bullet press with titles like "The Only Ten Flies You'll Ever Need" and "The Frugal Fly Box: Six That Do It All!" I devoured every such article. I wanted to keep things as simple as possible. The fewer the flies I could get away with, the better.

Naturally, then, I quickly developed a fondness for the Adams dry fly, famed wherever flies are fished for its desirability to trout even though it doesn't specifically imitate any of the bugs they regularly eat. The Adams became the fly I used the most. It seemed to me a damned near perfect thing, a fly that possessed the very essence of woodsy, streamy bugginess, of floating, drifting, bobbing, quivering, twitching, tasty-to-a-trout insectitude. There have been many variations of the Adams since Leonard Hallady tied the first one in Michigan in 1922, but the version I used was the common modern one made with black thread, grizzly hackle-tip wings, mixed brown and grizzly hackle fibers for the tail, muskrat dubbing, and mixed brown and grizzly hackle at the wings. It didn't take me long to learn that, while there were definitely times when only an imitation of a particular natural fly would induce a trout to strike, the percentage of the time that a properly presented Adams would do the job was extremely high.

An Adams, size 14, was the fly that ultimately worked when I had my first real one-on-one with a good brown trout. It was early evening, late May, in a peaceful little side pool on my stretch of the upper Beaverkill. The trout was rising to sip duns—I never did determine what fly they were—in a strand of current moving along the edge of a boulder at just the speed browns love to dine in. I couldn't be sure what size the fish was, but I knew it was bigger, and a lot more selective, than those tasty little brookies I'd caught one after another on the

Warner River in New Hampshire. Before I tried the Adams, the trout ignored several different flies I offered it, but didn't stop feeding. Then I tied on the Adams and with a short cast set it down a couple of feet up-current of the trout. It came floating along the boulder, hugging it, and the trout came up and took it, and I set the hook.

What a thrill! There are these moments in fly fishing, many of them, that suck you in another level deeper and guarantee that you will keep doing it as long as you are physically able and that you will never be able to live in a part of the country or the world where there are no trout rivers. (The company wants to move you from Schenectady to Palm Beach? No way!) Three or four minutes after setting the hook, I was holding in my hands a husky brown trout of at least thirteen inches, maybe fourteen, a muscular thug of a trout, a pissed-off bruiser, very well-fed. The great satisfaction I felt came not just from the catching of the fish but from the successful execution of the whole little drama, start to finish: the sighting of the feeding trout; the careful approach to get into good position and casting range; the first presentations that, though they did not catch the fish, did not spook it, either. Sometimes in dry-fly fishing, not putting a feeding trout down as it repeatedly rejects your flies is almost as gratifying as catching it.

Early experiences on the fertile pools of the big Beaverkill were just as exciting; in particular, matching Hendrickson hatches and green drake spinner falls. But I was saddened and put off by the scars on a couple of the fish I caught, which indicated that they'd been caught before, probably more than once, and abusively handled. This reinforced my preference for fishing in the less popular places, even if it meant catching fewer, less impressive fish.

My commitment to the Adams only grew when I read the late Art Lee's 1983 book, *Fishing Dry Flies for Trout on Rivers and Streams*. Lee describes an outing with the noted Catskill angler Ed Van Put in the tail of Cairn's Pool on the Beaverkill—Cairn's Eddy, he calls it, using the regional term for "pool"—during which Van Put hooks a "dozen or so nice fish" using a size 14 Adams. He writes that the Adams was one of the very few dry-fly patterns Van Put used. "If you want to say trout are selective, okay, *say they're selective about presentation*," Lee (his italics) quotes Van Put as saying. "But, about fly pattern, no way."

—❦—

When I wasn't fishing, I often hung out in Roscoe, to the extent one can hang out in such a small place. I killed time in the Little Store, an old-fashioned, wood-floored country department store, now defunct, that sold all sorts of wonderful outdoor merchandise, including trout flies and basic fishing tackle; the Beaverkill Angler fly shop across the street, whose proprietor, when I asked him if anyone had turned in my lost fly rod, gave me one of the shop's rods to use and said just to bring it back when I could; and the Roscoe Diner, famous pit stop for generations of students traveling on Route 17 between the New York City area and the upstate colleges whose pennants cover its walls. Sometimes I'd have a few beers at the Fairway Inn, also defunct, which was adjacent to Roscoe's rustic nine-hole golf course. One afternoon at the bar, I eavesdropped on a couple of older fellers in grubby work clothes—they looked as if they'd been baling hay all day—as they recounted with groans and laughs, mostly groans, what they'd really been doing: playing golf.

Roscoe may be prominent in the fly-fishing world—a sign welcomes drivers exiting Route 17 to TROUT TOWN USA—but in most respects it is a typical upstate hamlet: old, worn, resilient, civic-minded, friendly. There isn't much to keep you there long if you're not a fly fisher, or perhaps shopping for the person in your life who is. One year in the 1980s, I watched the Memorial Day parade: two or three old vets, one or two young ones, a few drummers from the high school, some Scouts, a vintage car, an old fire truck, an ambulance. I estimated the whole thing to be about fifty yards long, if that. There was considerable excitement when a woman fainted.

But for me at that time, tiny, quiet Roscoe was one of the places I most wanted to be. I never had to explain myself or my avocation there because it was the town where fly fishing ruled. The company was always sympathetic. It seemed that everyone—the waitresses in the diner, the people working in the shops, the bartenders, the old-timer sitting on the bench on Stewart Avenue—was at least familiar with fly fishing and understood its importance to the hamlet, even if he or she didn't do it. In Roscoe you could walk around in your chest waders (not that I ever did, or would) and no one would look twice. Roscoe was the home of the Dettes—Walt, Winnie, and their daughter, Mary—makers *par excellence* of elegant trout flies in the time-honored Catskill style. Their peers Elsie and Harry Darbee, until their deaths in 1980 and 1983, respectively, had lived a few miles out of town on Old Route 17. The angling superstars Joan and Lee Wulff lived in nearby Lew Beach and ran a fly-fishing school there. Numerous others who managed to squeeze at least part of a living out of fly fishing lived in the immediate area. For a dedicated fly fisherman like me, there was always a fine feeling in Roscoe of being right where the talent, the knowledge, and the history were, as well as a lot of people who were as crazy for it all as I was.

One afternoon very early in my Roscoe-going years, I walked into the Antrim Lodge just as a meeting of some civic or business group was breaking up. Walt Dette, a cardinal figure in a fly-tying tradition going back to Theodore Gordon, that Catskill fly fisherman of the late nineteenth and early twentieth centuries now known as the "father" of American dry-fly fishing, was sitting at a table all by himself, smoking a cigarette. I hadn't been to his fly shop yet, but I recognized him from photos. As a measure of my priorities in those days (not that they've changed), suffice it to say that it was a far more memorable moment for me than the time I found myself face-to-face with Mick Jagger at the Pyramid Club in Manhattan. No contest.

I was very fortunate that the Antrim, as of this writing long shuttered, was still open in those years. The Antrim's bar had a colorful history, going back to the 1920s, as a gathering place for fly fishermen, the celebrated as well as the anonymous. I came to it late, but you know what they say. Sometimes when I was there, I would think of Faulkner's description, in his story "The Bear," of hunting-camp talk as "the best of all talking." On a good night at the Antrim, I felt the same way about fishing talk. Real fly fishermen, no matter what they do in the nonfishing part of their lives, no matter how serious or important or engrossing it may be, literally can hardly stop talking about their sport once they get started.

That's how it was some nights at the Antrim bar: no business talk, no money talk, no politics or football or baseball; just hour after hour of brown trout, brook trout, rainbow trout, rivers, pools, riffles, rods, reels, graphite, bamboo, fiberglass, lines, knots, casting, hauling, hatches, duns, spinners, dry flies, wet flies, streamers, stone flies, nymphs, midges, hackle, dubbing, vises, Montana, Idaho, Michigan, Maine, Pennsylvania, Argentina, strategies, philosophies, points of view, weather, seasons, waders, wading boots, wading staffs, nets, vests, books, articles, stories, anecdotes, gossip, personalities. Then when you were finally too tired or had had a little too much beer and wanted to be on the stream by six in the morning, you could go upstairs to your spartan but comfortable old-time twenty-dollar room, bathroom down the hall, and conk out and dream about all the same stuff.

But my fishing excursions in those years weren't limited to Roscoe and the Beaverkill. Sometimes I had the use of a car and was able to explore more of the Catskill trout country, driving up and over the mountains through dot-on-the-map communities like Beaverkill, Lew Beach, and Turnwood on the higher-up Beaverkill; Claryville on the Neversink; Debruce and Willowemoc on the "Willow." Up there, well away from the main highways, there were still lightly used two-lane blacktops; old farmsteads with sagging barns; and gorgeous green prospects of fields, hills, and orchards, barely blemished by the twentieth century. It was deeply rural, at night old-world dark and silent. You could almost be fooled into thinking that little had changed since the days eighty years earlier when Theodore Gordon himself traveled to the upper Beaverkill on fishing tramps. It seemed far removed even from Roscoe, which since the 1960s has been cut through by the Route 17 "Quickway," a noisy expressway that runs both along and over parts of the Willowemoc and the big Beaverkill, inflicting huge esthetic damage and in places tormenting those anglers who equate fly fishing with peace and quiet.

I cast my flies in the Neversink, the Rondout, the Esopus, the West Branch of the Delaware, and the lower East Branch; in Fir Brook, Biscuit Brook, and brooks whose names I didn't know. I developed a lasting affection for the Willowemoc, the Beaverkill's smaller, less illustrious, less fished sibling, especially for the brook trout water in its upper reaches. Once I spent six humiliating hours getting skunked on the Schoharie, well known as the home stream of the late Art Flick of West Kill, whose study of its insect life resulted in his short but indispensable book, *A Streamside Guide to Naturals and Their Imitations*. As a Catskill angler—for that's what I was in the process of becoming in those years, a member of that particular school and tradition of fly fishing, more decidedly so with each passing year—I long made a point of going through Flick's book again before the start of each new season.

I loved wandering over and around the mountains for three or four days at a time, spending one day here, one day there, everything I needed in the trunk of the car, the purpose of each day being only to fish and to walk rivers and to think about fishing and rivers. At night

I'd find a bar in some fishing town like Phoenicia or Hancock and have a few drinks, just a serious fisherman passing through. As often as not I'd get my sleep in the car at a fishermen's parking area.

Sometimes I had a daydream in which I didn't have to work—wasn't rich, necessarily, but didn't have to work—and could live like this permanently, as a sort of full-time wandering angler, a total drop-out from conventional life, which it was becoming increasingly clear I didn't care for that much anyway. In this daydream I'd go to a place like Hunter or Prattsville and fish the Schoharie for a few days, and hang out a little at night, and then move on to another place—Livingston Manor, say, for the Willow, or Deposit for the West Branch of the Delaware, or Lake Placid in the Adirondacks for the West Branch of the Ausable. Or maybe I'd swing west out to Cooke City, Montana, to fish the Lamar and the Soda Butte in Yellowstone, and then over to Last Chance, Idaho, for the Henry's Fork, and then down to Basalt, Colorado, for the Roaring Fork and the Fryingpan. Maybe I'd have a small camper, or maybe I'd just stay in motels or pitch a tent at campsites. If it wasn't for my allergy, I'd have a dog or a cat. The years and the decades would pass, and I'd just keep crisscrossing the country and become a well-known angling eccentric. Fishermen would tell in bars of having run into me on the Metolius in Oregon, the Fox in the Upper Peninsula, Deep Creek in the Smokies. Usually I'd be agreeable with them, but sometimes I'd enforce the distance due a crank. I'd get old and older and finally I'd die, probably by slipping on some streamside stones and banging my head, or being carried away by a current that my younger legs would have easily handled.

In reality, of course, it wouldn't be so great an existence, not to mention useful or productive or of any significant worth to any other person or cause. But it was just a daydream, a fantasy, and there were times when I was down on the world and humankind when it seemed to me a perfectly sane and even rather beautiful way to live out a life.

CHAPTER THREE

The Town and the river—Where I
fished—The haunted Pepacton—
A place once defiled—A.J. McClane

MY NEW TOWN, MARGARETVILLE, WAS AN HONEST, UNASSUMING, agreeably no-frills sort of place. There wasn't even a McDonald's for more than twenty miles. Actually, I use the word "town" rather loosely: In the New York State system of local governance, Margaretville is not a town but a village, one of eight small communities that together compose the Town of Middletown (no relation to the distant city of Middletown, New York, down in Orange County). The town covers ninety-seven square miles in the southeast corner of Delaware County, which in turn covers almost fifteen hundred square miles, making it bigger than Rhode Island. Three-quarters of the county is forested. When I moved there in 1990, Delaware County's official population was 47,225, an increase of exactly 1,729 over 1890. This is not a part of the United States you go to for bright lights and fast times.

Things have changed a little since 1990, but in those days, when you pulled off Route 28 and drove over the Bridge Street Bridge into Margaretville's business district, you saw a Citgo station on your left and a big parking lot on your right. Retail businesses lined two sides of the parking lot, including an A&P, a Brooks Pharmacy, the Soap 'n' Suds laundromat, the Now & Then video-rental shop, and, fronting on Bridge Street, the Bun 'n' Cone diner. At the Bun 'n' Cone, Bridge

Street swept abruptly upward and met Main Street at the village's only traffic light.

A right turn on Main took you past the Village Pub, Del-Sports (guns and fishing gear), Wilson's Plumbing & Electrical Supply, B&D Motors (used cars, auto repair), the American Legion hall, and the *Catskill Mountain News*, among others, and quickly out of town on your way up Route 30 toward the village of Roxbury, almost twelve miles north.

A left turn took you past the small Department of Motor Vehicles office (no long lines in this one), Miller's Drug Store, the Margaretville Liquor Store, the Binnekill Square Restaurant, the Ming Moon Kitchen Chinese restaurant, a Victory Market, the Bull Run Tavern, a Sunoco station–cum–minimart, the Margaretville Central School, and the post office, among others, and on out along the East Branch toward the Pepacton Reservoir on County Highway 3, which roughly parallels Route 28 on the other side of the river.

If, though, after turning left at the light you took a quick right at Walnut Street and started driving away from Main Street, past the Fairview Public Library and the Hynes Funeral Home, and then bore left, you would soon be making a long, steady climb up Margaretville Mountain Road, higher and higher and higher still until you were far above the village. Then, having reached the crest, you'd be coasting downhill just as steeply, heading toward the photogenic New Kingston Valley and the tiny hamlet of New Kingston, where you might have the strange feeling you had just time-traveled back to the early twentieth century.

When I arrived in Margaretville, there was still an old-fashioned department store on Main Street selling everything from paper clips to winter boots, but before long it closed. And any description of Main Street must include the Galli-Curci Theater, named for Amelita Galli-Curci, the famous coloratura soprano who had an estate in nearby

Highmount and sang in the theater on its opening night in 1922. The theater had long served as a movie house but was now being used as a consignment shop for antiques and all kinds of old merchandise.

There was also a commercial strip along Route 28, which included a Red Barrel gas station and convenience store, Margaretville Bowl (eight lanes), Margaretville Memorial Hospital, Brookside Hardware (which also sold used cars and trucks), and the previously mentioned Inn Between Restaurant.

One of the first things people always ask about Margaretville is: Who was Margaret? I wish the answer were more interesting than it is. I wish I could say that Margaret was the flamboyant madam of a nineteenth-century bordello on Orchard Street, or a child of early settlers who was kidnapped by American Indians and raised by them before being swapped back for a couple of flintlock rifles and a sack of sugar. In reality, Margaret was a fancy girl: the daughter of Morgan Lewis, the third governor of New York, and, far more important, a member on her mother's side of the plutocratic Livingston family, which owned vast acreage in the Catskills at a time when the region was opening up for settlement and economic development. Margaret received the land on which the village is situated as an inheritance from her mother, Gertrude Livingston Lewis. Originally called Middletown Center, the village was officially named for Margaret when it incorporated in 1875, ninety-one years after the first permanent settlers of the site had put down their roots.

Those first settlers were Dutch pioneers from the Hudson Valley, near Kingston. Actually, the Dutch had tried to settle in the area twenty-one years earlier, in 1763, but were eventually chased off by American Indians. After the Revolutionary War they came back for another try. At the time, wolves, mountain lions, and elk, all ultimately forced out of the Catskill Mountains, still roamed them, and there were immense flocks of the now-extinct passenger pigeon.

Of course, Indigenous people had been present in the East Branch valley for centuries, probably since deep in prehistory, though they don't seem to have established many long-term settlements there. The word "Pakatakan" derives from the name of a seasonal American Indian village that was not far from the site of my cabin. The Iroquoian-speaking Mohawk Indians, who dominated a large region to the north, hunted and fished along both branches of the Delaware. The Algonquian-speaking Lenni Lenape Indians—or, more specifically, one of their three tribal divisions, the Munsee—bumped up against the Mohawks in this area, the East Branch more or less marking their northernmost range. The European pioneers called the Lenni Lenape the Delaware Indians, after the great river in whose valley the Lenape dwelt all the way south to Delaware Bay. (The English had named the river for the first royal governor of Virginia, Thomas West, third Baron De La Warr.)

After the war of 1775-83, the area that soon became Delaware County continued to be settled by people from other parts of the East—many of them were farmers from Connecticut looking for more space and better opportunity—and by emigrants from the British Isles and Continental Europe. By the middle of the nineteenth century, Margaretville was a thriving little hub of a few hundred souls where farmers came to take care of their business. It even had a hotel on Main Street.

Dairy farming had become the main form of agriculture in the county and in Middletown, and it would shape everything about the region—its economy; its culture; its big, rolling landscape strewn with cows, pastures, barns, silos, tractors, hayfields, cornfields, horses, stone walls, muddy pickup trucks—for more than a century and a half to come. Margaretville also became, for the first half or so of the twentieth century, a cauliflower capital; to this day there is a Cauliflower Festival in the village every fall.

50

But by the time I showed up to fish the East Branch, dairy farming in the area was well into its long decline. It was still the dominant form of agriculture, still a powerful social and cultural force, but the number of farms was shrinking every year as changing market conditions made it increasingly difficult for family-owned farms to stay in business. The ubiquitous old barns were sagging and collapsing or being torn down. Dairy farmers were retiring or finding other work and selling off large tracts of their land. A new kind of economy was taking form around the new occupants of much of that land: the part-time occupants, the second-homers whose primary residences were elsewhere, mainly close to or in New York City. As some of the farmers themselves put it, second homes were "the last crop."

— ⁓ —

About fifteen miles north of Margaretville on Route 30, on the other side of Roxbury, drivers going toward the hamlet of Grand Gorge soon see in the distance a notch in the mountains that looks like an enormous, wide-angled V. This is the Grand Gorge gap. The highway goes right through it.

Some sixteen thousand years ago, in the waning millennia of the last North American glaciation, a glacier situated north of the gap was melting. The meltwater became an icy lake that eventually started flowing through the notch and out the other side as a powerful, churning river, broad, deep, and fast. Today's normally peaceable East Branch is what remains of that mighty ancestor. Its headwaters, once a glacial lake, are now a string of inconspicuous wetland ponds lying beside Route 30.[1]

It's a little more than twenty miles from there to the Pepacton Reservoir, and as the East Branch makes this mostly north-south journey, picking up water from numerous tributaries along the way, it is slow to become a halfway decent trout stream. There are public-access fishing areas in the river's uppermost miles, between the headwaters and Roxbury, but the water in these areas is unlikely to interest serious fly anglers. This is good water for dozing by on a lazy summer afternoon. Roxbury, the first community the river reaches, was the hometown of both John Burroughs, the naturalist, essayist, philosopher, and Walt Whitman pal, and Jay Gould, the railroad magnate and financier who was one of the so-called robber barons of the nineteenth century; they were schoolmates. As the East Branch goes through Roxbury and then toward the hamlet of Halcottsville, it is alternately in and out of view from the Route 30 highway. In Halcottsville there is an impoundment, called Lake Wawaka, that was built long ago to generate power for mills and electricity but is now used by canoeing and kayaking tourists.

At the small settlement of Kelly Corners, a few miles downstream of Halcottsville, the East Branch gets a good boost from the Batavia Kill tributary; and then, just a half mile outside Margaretville proper, it meets and absorbs the substantial flow of Dry Brook.[2] Thus bulked up, it makes a southerly swing from Route 30 to Route 28 and proceeds through town, now running basically southwest before being interrupted by the Pepacton Reservoir three to four miles farther on.

I didn't fish the river upstream of Margaretville more than a half-dozen times. I'm not even qualified to comment on it. Nor was I drawn to the water within the village except when, for whatever reason, it was the only convenient way to get my fishing in. I knew there were some fine trout in that water, but municipal fishing, even in a burg of only 639 people, was not what I was there for.

In my six full seasons on the upper East Branch, most of my fishing by far was done on the part of the river that runs between the village and the reservoir, a distance of about three highway miles. Much of this water is not visible from the road. The woods, fairly deep in places, create a screen on both sides of the river. Depending on your access point, a little effort may be required to get to the stream. This is Bureau of Water Supply property, owned by the City of New York, 140 miles away, and permanently protected from development. In order to fish there, I had to get a permit (free) from the city's Department of Environmental Protection.

I quickly grew very fond of this mostly gentle, winding, wandering woodland water, even before I had much of an idea how it was going to fish. In size it was about the same as my old stretch of the upper Beaverkill. Like that water, it was wide open to the sky and the sun in some places and narrow, tight, heavily canopied in others. But it was much less rocky than the upper Beaverkill, with few boulders in the river or along the bank; when you needed a place to sit to change your rig or have a snack or recover from the pain of losing a good fish, the bank itself usually had to do, unless a downed tree was available. The streambed, mostly small stones, gravel, and silt, made for generally easy wading.

There were some short but deep pools and runs where, had I been the serious nympher then that I later became, I would have spent far more time than I did, trying to catch the big brownies that, as I did eventually learn, were sometimes lurking there down on the bottom. (Only when I overcame my long aversion to deep nymphing and made a total commitment to learning it did I start to discover the thrilling secrets that rivers keep.) There were several old beaver homes and numerous fly-snagging deadfalls, a few of them reaching across most of the river. There were places where currents broke off abruptly to either side of the stream and spilled down the gradient in sweetly hissing riffles that fell into little black or sea-green plunge pools where a ten-inch trout would smash a 16 Adams or Elk Hair Caddis the moment it landed, and others where the breakaway current swept into and around a deep bend in the cutout bank and backed up into itself, creating a pocket of slack, undulating, irresistible dry-fly water and sometimes a brown, slowly turning, scary-looking whirlpool. The surface around the whirlpool would be covered with thick, coffee-colored foam that was clogged with a downstream-drifting debris of leaves, twigs, and bugs. The bugs, if not already dead, were at serious risk from below.

Two of these runaway currents, the second a few hundred feet downstream of the first, swung left (looking downstream) away from the river and then, after the first had made a big loop, joined up and became what was in effect a separate trout stream running adjacent to the main river on the far side of the bank. As a result, for a long distance—the two streams ultimately did reconnect—I had two trout rivers in one. I had some good fishing on this bonus river and often spent an entire outing on it. Other times I would spend a few hours on the main river and then climb up on the high bank and make my way through the chest-high grasses and the thickets of trees and the deer beds to spend a few more hours on the other stream.

I fished this water between the village and the reservoir well more than three hundred times, and so rarely did I even glimpse another angler from afar, let alone meet up with one, that it always came as a jolt when I did. Normally it was just me and the critters: lots of deer, of course; coyotes, I assume—I never saw them out there (I did near my cabin), but I heard them occasionally at sundown; muskrats; porcupines; bobcats, no doubt; a snapping turtle or two; herons; mergansers; mallards; hawks; once in a while an eagle. The Catskill forest is loaded with bears, but I never saw one along the East Branch.

As for the reservoir, I never fished it. It is famous for its humongous brown trout, and every season the *Catskill Mountain News* (which ceased publication in 2020 after more than a century) ran photos of bait fishermen and spin fishermen posing proudly with these toothy wall-hangers of the deep, many of which are caught with sawbellies. But this just wasn't my kind of fishing. I did rivers and streams with flies, and that was pretty much it. By the time I got to Margaretville, I hardly knew what to do anymore with water that wasn't moving.

—❦—

The Pepacton—the name is believed to come from an American Indian word for "marriage of the waters"—extends about twenty-one basically east-west road miles from the hamlet of Dunraven, just west of Margaretville, to the dam at Downsville. In volume it is the biggest of New York City's nineteen reservoirs, providing about twenty-five percent of the city's water. It went into service in 1955, its construction having consumed a quarter of the original East Branch. Its shape, if that word can even be used, is a long, horizontal squiggle, like something a toddler might draw with a crayon. At its widest point it is a little more than a half mile across. Surrounded by forest, far from population centers of any size, the Pepacton is undeniably beautiful during the green, sunny months of the Catskill summer, no less so at night as it gleams beneath a bright moon and a clear, starry sky.

It is also, like many reservoirs, haunted. The City of New York, using the power of eminent domain, condemned and razed four small communities in order to build it, wiping out farms, houses, businesses, post offices, schools, and churches. Almost a thousand people were displaced—some of them moved to Margaretville—as were those who lay in their cemeteries, who were reinterred elsewhere. In drought years, when the reservoir shrinks and its floor becomes increasingly exposed, the remains of the lost settlements—Arena, Shavertown, Union Grove, and Pepacton—begin to appear: rusting farm tools, sections of sidewalk and road.

A citizen of Shavertown at the time wrote a poem that included these lines[3]:

> Man's home was once his castle,
> He's seen it torn to shreds;
> The hallowed place where once it stood
> Will be the river's bed.
> A battered, plundered, smoking ruin,
> Oh for eyes that cannot see
> Or ears that cannot hear
> Or feel, this endless misery.

Of course, the residents of these communities weren't the only ones who lost their homes and ways of life to the water needs of the distant metropolis. The same thing happened when the City built its other Catskill-region reservoirs: the Ashokan (the first, put into service in 1915), the Schoharie, the Rondout, the Neversink, and the Cannonsville. The Neversink Reservoir submerged the place where Theodore Gordon himself had lived, though Gordon was not a native of the region.

Driving the length of the Pepacton between Dunraven and Downsville, a trip one can make without seeing more than three or four other vehicles, I've often tried to picture what the East Branch valley looked like before it was flooded. Old photos and postcards give us a good idea: nineteenth-century farmsteads, covered bridges, unpaved roads, dairy cows, mills, creameries, tree-lined village streets, hitching posts, general stores, schoolhouses, little girls in sailor dresses, little boys in knickerbockers, oxen, draft horses, buckboards, vintage automobiles, service stations, boarding houses, hotels, barn raisings, picnics—all the iconography of an earlier, agrarian, often romanticized way of American life.

The novel *When You Live by a River*, by the Catskills-based writer Mermer Blakeslee, is a beautifully imagined, close-up look at that life in 1931: the milk houses, smokehouses, and outhouses; the relentlessly stony Delaware County soil; the women wearing skirts sewn from feed sacks; the homemade corn liquor; the whistles of the trains of the Delaware & Northern Railroad following the course of the river between Arkville, the hamlet adjoining Margaretville to the east, and the village of East Branch, where the river of the same name merges with the Beaverkill. The story takes place mostly in Pepacton, where the East Branch "spread out brown and slow, like a big old leg thrown over the valley." Surveyors and officials from New York City have started showing up in the area. The farmers and townsfolk are trying to come to terms with the astonishing fact that the East Branch, "something with its own power and will and life," is going to be "stoppered up," and their houses burned, their land inundated, their dead moved to other cemeteries. Of one of her characters, a farmer deep in grief over the loss of his young wife in childbirth, Blakeslee writes: "The river smell always brought him some relief. As if his soul, like the East Branch, reached all the way up to the headwaters in Grand Gorge, and downriver, too, through Peaceful Valley and into Shinhopple until just west of Fishs Eddy,[4] where it gave itself to the Delaware. There, at the junction, he seemed to end."

John Burroughs left us a rather sidelong but subtly evocative account of that lost world—an earlier version of it than Blakeslee's—in his essay "Pepacton: A Summer Voyage," which appeared in *The Atlantic Monthly* in 1880. The essay recounts a journey Burroughs took down the East Branch, commonly known then as the Pepacton Branch, in a boat he built expressly for the trip. His destination was Hancock, some fifty miles away, where the East Branch and the West Branch meet. Burroughs took his boat by train to Arkville and put in there in Dry Brook, which he drifted to its junction with the East

Branch. On his voyage through the valley, Burroughs asks for milk at farmhouses and feasts in fields of wild strawberries. Cattle "ruminating leg-deep in the water" turn and run when they see his boat coming, "as if they had seen a spectre." Burroughs surprises a group of schoolgirls "with skirts amazingly abbreviated, wading and playing in the water," and meets two young Huck Finns who are navigating the river on crude rafts; they climb aboard his boat and travel with him awhile. He takes shelter from a rainstorm at the covered bridge in Shavertown, observing the "unpainted houses and barns of the Shavertowners." He surprises "an ancient fisherman seated on a spit of gravelly beach," prompting the old fellow to get up and hurry away. "I presume," Burroughs writes, "he had angled there for forty years without having his privacy thus intruded upon."

You don't have to live in or around Margaretville long before you sense the deep resentment of New York City that many people still carry in their hearts, and it isn't just because of the memory of what was taken so that the Pepacton could be built.

It's also because the City, authorized by the state to regulate land use in the watershed to keep its drinking water safe from contamination, plays a permanent, powerful, and often adversarial role, regulatory and economic, in local affairs. Residents complain about onerous, costly, time-consuming regulations that can make it hard to expand a house or grow a business. The Pepacton's water, like the water in all the Catskill-region reservoirs, goes to New York City unfiltered, and constant pressure from the federal government to maintain its purity or be required to build a hugely expensive filtration plant has only intensified the City's water-protection efforts. (The water does get treated with chlorine and fluoride and go through ultraviolet disinfection.) One of the City's main strategies has been to purchase many thousands of acres of land around the reservoir and its feeder streams to keep the land undeveloped. Local people say that this further reduces the possibility of economic growth in an area chronically desperate for it.

Fly fishermen and others who have a strong personal investment in the environment may have conflicted feelings about the reservoir's history, but the awkward fact is that we gain immensely from the City's need to keep the Catskill rivers and reservoirs clean and its policy of buffering them with forever-wild land. I'd be a phony if I pretended not to love the No ADMITTANCE EXCEPT TO FISHERMEN sign that welcomed me when I entered the pristine City-owned woods wherein lay my favorite stretch of the upper East Branch. (The signs have changed since then, but that place is still fishing-only; other activities are allowed on other City-owned land.) As we cast our flies for trout in a clear, sparkling, insect-rich Catskill stream today, it is almost impossible to comprehend the environmental ruin that humans once inflicted on these mountains and rivers. Beginning around the start of the nineteenth century and continuing into the twentieth, lumbering, countless mills of various kinds, the leather-tanning industry, and the so-called acid factories greedily stripped the mountains of white pines, hemlocks, and hardwoods and dumped leavings, toxic wastes, and industrial poisons directly into the rivers.

The tanneries were filthy, stinking places that treated animal hides with tannic acid, part of the process of turning them into leather. The tannic acid came from tannins extracted from hemlock bark. In addition to hemlock trees, the tanneries required a steady supply of water for both the tanning process and the removal of waste and effluent, and the trout rivers provided it. At the industry's peak there were more than sixty tanneries situated on Catskill rivers, including at

Margaretville and Dunraven (then called Clark's Factory, the "factory" being the tannery). But by the late nineteenth century, they'd all gone out of business, having used up all the available hemlocks.

The acid factories, which followed upon the disappearing tanneries, weren't as many in number but might have been even worse for the environment. They used hardwoods like maple, oak, ash, and birch to manufacture wood alcohol, acetate of lime, creosote, charcoal, and other wood derivatives. Again, their poisonous wastes went straight into the Catskill rivers, leaving long stretches of water uninhabitable for fish and other aquatic life. The closest acid factories to Margaretville were in Arkville and Shavertown. It's hard to believe, but the last Catskill acid factory, on the hallowed Beaverkill at Horton, didn't close until after World War II. Fly fishermen today know the water near the site as Acid Factory Run, a fine place to fish now but certainly not one of the more bucolic names in angling geography.

On his journey down the East Branch, John Burroughs, a devoted trout fisherman all his long life, sees fish scattering from his boat's shadow "like chickens when a hawk appears." He doesn't say what kind of fish they are, but if they were trout, they would have had to be native brookies, since brown and rainbow trout had not yet been introduced in the Catskills. What's more likely, though, is that they were smallmouth bass, a species for which the East Branch was well known at the time.

The previously mentioned Ed Van Put, who is not only an angler of high repute but also a retired state fisheries professional and a historian of Catskill fly fishing, explains in his exhaustively researched book *Trout Fishing in the Catskills* how brown trout, after their introduction into the East Branch in the 1880s, gradually displaced bass in the upper reaches of the river, where the cooler water suited them better than it did the bass. They reduced the brook trout to second-class citizens as well. By the 1920s the East Branch in and near Margaretville, especially parts of the river eventually consumed by the reservoir, had become known as the home of brown trout exceeding five, six, even seven pounds in weight and two feet in length—leviathans the likes of which can now be caught only in the deep, alewives-rich water of the reservoir. Van Put found a 1931 newspaper account of a brownie caught near Arena that allegedly weighed ten pounds and measured thirty inches.

This was the river that awaited Albert Jules McClane when he made his way to the area at the advanced age of thirteen. It was the Depression, and young Al, who'd been raised in Brooklyn and Queens and was already an experienced fisherman, was looking for work. He found it on a dairy farm, the first of a number of hard physical jobs he would have in the Margaretville area in his teens. When he wasn't working, he pursued his fishing education on the East Branch and its tributaries. Many years later, when he had become arguably the preeminent fishing writer of his time, McClane wrote that in the Margaretville of his early years, "Even getting a tooth pulled during a mayfly hatch was impossible. Our only dentist, Doc Faulkner, would be on the river. Doc once broke his leg and was wading the next day in a plaster cast."[5]

Doc Faulkner was one of the local men, both resident and visiting, among whom the boy found friends and fishing mentors. Another was the outdoor writer John Alden Knight, best known today as the creator of the Solunar Tables. But the most important of this group for McClane was Dan Todd, the Margaretville stationmaster for the old Ulster and Delaware Railroad. As a fly fisherman, McClane would write, Todd was "the purist of purists." His assistant stationmaster,

Ray Neidig, was also immersed in the angling life, and their station house "looked more like a tackle shop than what it was."

McClane wrote about a lesson he learned from Todd one July evening when they were fishing "the Arkville flat of the Bushkill." Todd had shown him that the key to catching trout that night was "the fat reddish-brown caddisflies that hatched in the weeds at dusk" and "were running up and down the reed stems and depositing their eggs in the water," a phenomenon obvious to Todd but invisible to the apprentice. "On the way home that night Dan said that someday I might make a fly fisherman," McClane wrote, "but first I had to observe stream life rather than just look at it."

It was on the East Branch in Margaretville, on a cold, snowy day in April, that McClane, at age fourteen, caught his first really huge trout. He took it on a nymph cast upstream. "The trout was too big for my landing net," he wrote years later, "and I remember, after getting its head stuck in the mesh, wrestling my prize into a snowbank. I walked home, feeling like one big goose pimple, by way of the lumberyard, the butcher shop, the drugstore, and the ill-named Palace Hotel, making sure everybody in town saw my fish. Dan Todd weighed it at the railroad station—7 pounds, 2 ounces, not an adult trophy for the East Branch in those days, since fresh mounts in double figures to 15 pounds or more hung glassy-eyed on every saloon wall."

Young Al—he adopted "A.J." for byline purposes only after his writing career had begun—also enjoyed fishing for brook trout in a small, icy-cold, rather remote tributary of Dry Brook that ran through the forest in Rider Hollow, well upstream of Arkville. He would make a fire and cook his brookies in an iron skillet that he kept hidden away "under a granite ledge," and that, he reflected decades later, "must be an oxidized artifact today."

One of these days I'll have to go looking for that skillet.

NOTES

1. My main authority on the origins of the East Branch is Robert Titus, *The Catskills in the Ice Age*, revised ed. (Fleischmanns, NY: Purple Mountain Press, 2003), 79–83.

2. There is some disagreement over the name of this tributary. Local people call it Dry Brook, seeing it as a continuation of the stream of that name that comes into Arkville, a hamlet immediately east of Margaretville, from the south, and merges there with the Bush Kill coming in from the east. The sign at the bridge going over the stream on Route 28 says DRY BROOK. U.S. Geological Survey maps also identify the stream as Dry Brook. But the state Department of Environmental Conservation identifies this water as the Bush Kill. Since I have to choose one or the other, I'll keep Dry Brook.

3. I came upon this poem on page 144 of *Two Stones for Every Dirt: The Story of Delaware County, New York*, by the Delaware County Historical Association (Fleischmanns, NY: Purple Mountain Press, 1987). The DCHA's source was a clipping from the *Catskill Mountain News* in the Fleischmanns Museum of Memories. I've corrected the spelling of the original "shreads" to shreds.

4. That's right—no apostrophe in the name of this river hamlet.

5. The McClane articles from which this and the quoted material in the next four paragraphs are taken are, in order: "The Beautiful Dancer," "The Fish Jumped over a Spoon" (footnote), "Summer Trout," "Nymph Is Not a Dirty Word," and "Angling for Trout."

PART TWO

EAST BRANCH DAYS

As the nights grew colder that first fall, I did my best to insulate the cabin, which had not been built for winter comfort, against the coming deep freeze. I sealed off the windows with clear, heavy plastic and duct tape, and both the front door and the rarely used side door off the kitchen with felt weatherproofing, which I also put anywhere else I felt cold air coming in.

Still, by early January, when temperatures late at night and first thing in the morning were routinely in the single digits or below zero, the old propane heater was laboring nonstop just to keep the inside temperature around sixty. I didn't mind the temperature, but the sound of the heater constantly switching on was painful, because it was the sound of dollar bills burning—dollar bills I didn't have. I felt a little guilty one frigid morning when I saw the big white-and-red truck of the local fuel company backing into my driveway to make an unrequested propane delivery. I sure did let the nice man fill up my tank, though.

In an attempt to make my fuel last, I decided to keep both bedrooms closed off for the rest of the winter. I liked sleeping on the couch anyway, by the fireplace embers. Then I closed off the kitchen, too, by hanging a heavy quilt between it and the living room. A few mornings later the kitchen had become a walk-in freezer. The olive oil was frozen solid in its bottle, and when I wanted a beer, all I had to do was reach behind the quilt and grab a frosty one off the counter. Of course, the water in the pipes under the sink had also frozen—the first of many water-line freeze-ups I would have in the cabin—and had to be melted with an electric space heater.

But the living room was comfortable, at least to someone wearing long johns, a layer or two of warm clothing, and, sometimes, a knit hat. For each of my six winters in that cabin, the long johns went on before the end of September and didn't come off for good until well into April, about the time the quill Gordons were giving way to the Hendricksons. What a great day that always was! Life would have been a lot harder without my thermals.

Another issue was the cold coming up through the floor. To sit at my desk for any length of time was to feel it slowly moving up from the soles of my boots to my knees. The cure for this was the same electric space heater, which was of 1950s vintage and had been left behind by a previous tenant of one of my New York apartments. Placed at my feet, it kept the blood in my lower legs from going the way of the olive oil.

Years after leaving Margaretville, when I finally got around to reading the writings and letters of Theodore Gordon, I was interested to learn that even the father of American dry-fly fishing, who was better off than I but still had to watch his money, had had his off-season inconveniences down on the Neversink.

In the December 23, 1905, issue of the *Fishing Gazette*, a British journal for which Gordon long wrote, he said: "As I write, the wind is shrieking and tearing at this frail wooden house as if determined to carry it off bodily. The houses here are not adapted to the winter climate. Many of the rooms are closed and the family occupy only a few which can be kept fairly warm."

In the same publication on March 17, 1906: "This is the first winter I have spent far from the maddening crowd, in the real country, far from railroads and towns, and I admit that there has been considerable discomfort as well as pleasure. It is difficult to perform one's ablutions in solid ice, and getting out of bed in the morning is a decidedly shivery affair."

In the same dispatch, on how the coldness in his lodgings affected his fly tying: "For years I have used a vise, and was fully convinced that my clumsy fingers could not do the work alone. However, during the bitterly cold weather I could not work at a table near a window without freezing, and I could not read all the time, so was driven to try finger work as I sat almost on top of the wood-burning stove."

I didn't have a woodstove, unfortunately, but I did have a fine big fireplace and a large supply of quality firewood on the screened porch. I almost always had a blaze going. The raised hearth was great for warming cold feet while sitting back in a chair, and provided an extra, irresistible place for visitors to sit.

I knew that, technically, a fire actually lowers the temperature of a winter dwelling by consuming its air, but for me this fact was far outweighed by the spiritual, psychological, and esthetic benefits of a fire, which are huge. A good fire serves as a mood lifter, a sedative, a counselor, a therapist, a hypnotist, a time machine, a looking glass, all in one. If I watch TV for an hour, my brain often feels like a junkyard; if I watch a fire, it feels cleansed. And when you have a really good hardwood blaze going, there is a pocket of dry, toasty air within three or four feet of the hearth that will keep you warm even at thirty below. There were nights I cooked my dinner there.

It was from somewhere around the edges of the fireplace, late that February or early in March, that furry, slate-gray little creatures started sneaking into the cabin and making a beeline for the garbage can in the kitchen. At first I assumed they were mice, but after regrettably having to murder a few, I noticed that they had much sharper snouts than mice and the tiniest of eyes. My aging copy of *Animal Friends and Foes,* by Osmond P. Breland, informed me that they were shrews. It was my first encounter with these secretive, vile-tempered, incessantly hungry animals. "A shrew does not hesitate to attack a mouse or other animal more than twice its size, and it frequently manages to kill its larger opponent," Professor Breland writes.

But my shrews were no match for the little snap traps I bought at Brookside Hardware. I wonder if they were the same critters that ate my blue books.

For days at a time that first winter in Margaretville, I didn't talk with anyone. Then there were days, many of them, when my only conversations were with the counter people from whom I bought a newspaper or a cup of coffee when I walked into town or down the hill to the Red Barrel on Route 28, which became my main hangout. I wasn't one to send all my friends and acquaintances my new address and phone number every time I moved, and as a consequence, few people from my life in the city knew where I was. The old rotary phone on the kitchen wall rang so infrequently that when it did, I practically jumped out of my boots.

But I liked things the way they were. In those pre-Internet, pre-smartphone, pre-social-media days, you could still disappear, at least for a good long while. These days, no matter where you go, no matter how you may want to change your life, no matter how much privacy you may want or even be desperate for, anyone with a computer can track you down, tap you on the shoulder, make you explain yourself. It is an immeasurable loss. I did often yearn for my recent girlfriend back in the city, but that had died a natural, inevitable death anyway and I knew my yearnings were illusional, a function of so much isolation and silence.

Every once in a while, I ran into my only full-time neighbor up on the mountainside that winter, Bill. Bill was in his early seventies and lived in a small cabin, his retirement home, at the top of the dirt road. He told me he had spent forty years with a water company in New Jersey, retiring as assistant supervisor. Unfailingly friendly and generous, Bill was of medium build, with thinning white hair and a cheerful, ruddy, beaming face. He almost always wore a fedora, no matter the weather. He was a loner who didn't have a television or even a telephone. "Aw, Jesus, all those wires goin' into the house," he said to me more than once. "Nah, I don't like it." Bill enjoyed working in his yard, driving around town in his little Ford Ranger pickup, listening to his radio at night, and drinking beer. He had beautiful handwriting.

Since, unlike me, Bill didn't have to worry about money, his propane heater was always on and his cabin was nice and warm. It was pleasant to sit at his kitchen table with him on a winter afternoon and watch the snow come down and get buzzed on Milwaukee's Best. His cabin was furnished sort of like a motel room and was always immaculate, as if ready for the next guest. Everything was perfectly arranged, lined up, centered. All the surfaces were bare except for a few souvenir-type knickknacks, each of them thoughtfully, precisely placed. On the walls were a couple of woodsy scenes from the five-and-dime, as in my cabin. Enough of the bed was visible in the bedroom to see that the blanket was tucked in tight and smooth. The first time I was in Bill's cabin, there was an *Outdoor Life* magazine propped upright on the seat of an armchair, leaning against the back-rest, perfectly centered; Bill had turned it into decor. Bill smoked a lot of cigarettes, and you could tell which chair was his favorite because the ceiling above it was nicotine-stained.

Bill's pickup truck (two-tone brown—it reminded me of my sto-len tackle box) was as tidy inside as his cabin. He parked it out front by his tool shed, which had a copy of an animal's head—I think it was a wolverine, but was never sure—mounted over the door. Bill had put many such touches all over his property. A wooden sign nailed to a tree said BILL'S PLACE. Another sign on a tree bore the carved figure of a deer and said CAMP DEER RUB. There were several representa-tions of the American flag, some small statuary, some pots with plastic flowers, and, on a tree stump, a decorative cannon. Recently Bill had hung up wind chimes.

Bill and I enforced a friendly distance from each other during the years we were neighbors—one did not live in that place because one sought an engaged social life—but we became pretty good pals and would always help each other out in a pinch; for example, when there was a lot of shoveling to be done to liberate our vehicles from the most recent two-foot snowfall. Most of my memories of Bill seem to involve snow, of which there was a stupendous amount in the six winters I lived on that mountainside, waiting for trout season to come around again. In fact, it was with a foot or two of new snow on the ground, in bright moonlight, framed by hemlock boughs drooping deeply from snow weight, that my cabin looked its best, all lit up and cozy-seeming at the bottom of the snowfield sloping down from the road. It might have been fifty degrees inside, but it sure did *look* warm and cocoa-comfy.

For a great many people, trying to make ends meet in the rural Catskill Mountains, especially in winter, requires all the effort, resil-ience, and adaptability they can summon. I was now one of these people. Making things even harder in the very early nineties was that the United States was in a recession, though recession-like conditions are more or less normal in the Catskills anyway.

That first fall I called and visited businesses all over the region, especially restaurants, to see if I could get some part-time work. My needs were minimal—I was just a trout bum trying to make it to spring—and I wasn't fussy. But time after time I whiffed. "You've got a college degree," a man at a ski area said as he turned me down, looking at my application. "What do you want to make snow for?" That was the last time I made that mistake. For a while I ran a classified ad in the *Catskill Mountain News* basically availing myself to anyone for anything, but all it got me was two days of yard work for a wonderful old German couple in nearby Denver. Seven dollars an hour, I think it was, plus lots of tea and cookies.

Finally my fortunes picked up a bit. First I landed a regular Saturday-night shift washing dishes at the Emory Brook, a small, excellent restaurant and inn in the little village of Fleischmanns, five or six miles east of Margaretville. Originally called Griffin Corners, Fleischmanns was renamed for the well-known yeast family, at one time the village's most influential and benevolent residents. In the first half or so of the twentieth century, it flourished as a holiday destination, but the golden days of packed hotels and thronging vacationers were long gone, and it showed. Later in the nineties, the makers of the Christian Slater movie *Julian Po*, looking for a certain mood, filmed in Fleischmanns, taking full advantage of the down-at-the-heels backdrops they found in the heart of town.

I had never done any sort of work in a restaurant before, but my job at the Emory Brook was the first of several such jobs I would have during my time in Margaretville. In that bleak, heavily weekend economy, those were the jobs that were available. They served my purposes and needs, and no matter how menial the work, I liked having them, not just for the money but because they took me out of my mountainside isolation and put me among people, and also because there was always a free meal, usually a really good one, and then a free drink or two at the bar after the work was done. There was no better way to learn about the local sociology: who was who, who was in jail, who was fornicating with whom. Staff romances, or at least flings, developed easily. The turnover on kitchen and dining-room staffs was constant, and some of the cooks and waitresses seemed to have worked in just about every hash house in three counties and just kept cycling through.

Since I had my own maul and wedge for splitting firewood, my friends at the Emory Brook also hired me to split a large amount of maple logs they had on their property from the clearing of several trees. A valuable by-product of this work was all the first-rate firewood I was allowed to keep for my own fireplace. For me, firewood ranked just a notch below food in importance. It was almost as good as money. I was always quick to let people know that I had maul, would travel.

Then, through sheer persistence, I got some more work at a busy, sometimes rowdy roadhouse across from the old train station in Arkville, called Railz. (For some reason I still think of the pretty girl, barely high-school age, who walked up to the bar one night and said, "Was my mom in here last night? Was she trashed? Was she trashed?") The owner needed someone to wash dishes from time to time and to help him with various other jobs, including more wood splitting for the establishment's big, insatiable woodstove. I was happy to be on call.

As infrequent and irregular as these and a few other odd jobs I managed to scrape up were, they made all the difference financially and, almost as important, helped the long winter go by. Spiritually and psychologically, the arrival of March 1 was a major event that winter, as it would be every subsequent winter I lived in the cabin; it felt like a day to be celebrated, an unofficial holiday. It was still winter, still cold, still gray and raw and windy, and the snow still fell; but it was March—a mere month before the official start of trout season. Daylight was already appreciably longer. Early in the month there were three or four unusually mild days when I was able to keep the front door open—so as to *warm* the cabin—and to sit at the kitchen table again.

Never had I been more attentive to the incremental change from one season to the next as I was during that winter's slow dissolve into spring. There were afternoons of thaw that March when the sun had a long-absent warmth to it and, accompanied by the sound of Bill's wind chimes carrying through the trees, great blobs of snow parted from the hemlock boughs and crashed with heavy thuds onto the roof and with soft thuds into the yard, pocking the still-deep but slowly melting snow there. From the screened porch this very beginning of the melt-off of so much snow and ice sounded like paper being quietly crinkled. Then it became a loud, round-the-clock gurgling and running and dripping that was the very sound of liberation to my winter-weary bones and brain. The wind off the mountain persisted but lost its biting edge. At night there was more and more animal activity outside, the snarls and screeches of conflict as the woods came to life again. Even the appearance of tiny flies trapped between the windows and the clear plastic I'd covered them with six months earlier was a spiritual lift.

But Catskill winters seem not to want to let go. They fatally weaken, but then they cling, and cling, and cling. April 1 may be the opening day of trout season, but the weather is often so miserable that day, and the rivers so high and cold, that I've never bothered with it. Not until the last week or ten days of the month does the landscape start to change, the oppressive browns and grays and dirty whites of the mountainsides finally giving way to the palest, gauziest, most delicate "tender haze of green," as Theodore Gordon described it in the *Fishing Gazette*. This begins as but a mere exhalation of green, a baby's breath of green, easily overlooked by most people but eagerly awaited every day by those of us who just can't stand to miss this sort of thing. A few weeks later the forsythias are in full bloom and the grass, sprouting dandelions, needs a cutting.

I wish I could report that, having moved to trout country to surrender myself to my love of angling, I proceeded to have a glorious, sun-splashed, dreamlike first season on the East Branch, filled with unforgettable moments like the ones captured in the photos in the fishing magazines in which some grinning, cocksure, bandana-necked fisherman decked out in Simms and Patagonia holds a grotesquely obese brown or rainbow trout—a real "hawg," don't you know—up for the camera while manfully, albeit insufferably, gripping his nine-hundred-dollar fly rod between his teeth.

But it wasn't like that. It wasn't like that at all.

At first I was so thrilled just to be out there, alone on the river, invisible in the woods, a free man, that I didn't even care that much about how I was doing as a fisherman. Of the two people inside every true fly fisher—the undying boy or girl roaming the streams and the woods with a rod in hand, happy for that alone, contented; and the serious student of rivers, fish, insects, and angling, desirous of confirmation, success—I was much more the first that spring than the second. Sometimes, hiking through the trees on my way to the stream, not another soul in sight, most of my fellow citizens toiling honorably at work to help keep the world turning, I would think: *Well, I must be doing* something *right to be so blessed, and if this is to be my fate, this simple thing and nothing more, it's not bad at all as far as fates go.*

There was almost too much water to explore anyway, too much land to get the lay of, to become preoccupied with the numbers game of fishing. Even allowing for the time I was able to spend on the river before the close of the prior season, I was still new to this East Branch country, still seeing much of it for the first time. And there was so much other trout water nearby. I drove up to Delhi and Hamden to check out the West Branch along Route 10, and went down Route 28 to look over the upper parts of the Esopus. I even took long, covetous drives along the upper Dry Brook and Mill Brook, both in my general neighborhood but off-limits to public fishing—which made me a little crazy, so badly did I want at them.

But fishing was what I was there to do, and though it took a while to sink in, eventually I had to admit that I was doing it with a notable lack of success. In the city they would say I was stinking the joint up. That spring-into-summer, in particular, the best part of the fly-fishing season, was basically just a continuation of the poor outings I'd had on the East Branch after moving into the cabin the previous summer. I am not a competitive, ego-driven, greedy, aggressive, numbers-keeping, watch-me-kick-your-ass sort of fisherman, and would rather have a prostate biopsy than spend a day with anyone who is, either on or off the river; and I am as capable as anyone of appreciating a day astream for all the poetry and therapy it provides apart from the catching of fish. But I was getting mighty tired of eight- and nine-inch trout, and there were too many days when I was catching nothing at all. It was scary. What was happening?

I knew going in, of course, that in numbers and sizes of fish, this was not the Beaverkill or the Willowemoc or the tailwater East Branch below Downsville. That was part of the trade-off I had gladly made. Still, I'd been confident I would be able to catch more and better trout in the East Branch than I was now doing. Once or twice, succumbing to that same sort of frustration that makes a golfer throw his club into the pond (I've never seen a frustrated angler throw a fly rod, a much more complicated and probably expensive proposition, but I'm sure it's happened), I resorted to the stupidity of blaming the river, a mistake no clearheaded fisherman allows himself to make just because the river isn't bending to his will. Then as now, I firmly believed that if there is but a single fish in a river, the real angler finds it and figures out how to catch it.

No, the problem wasn't the river; it was the fisherman. It was the simple fact that I was not the fly fisherman I had fooled myself into thinking I was by the time I moved to Margaretville—which was, I'm amused to admit now, a pretty damned good one. I had worked long and hard on my basic skills: casting, presentation, mending, stealthy wading, reading the water, playing and releasing a fish. I'd raised and caught good trout on Hendricksons, March Browns, Green Drakes, and Coffin Flies on some of the fabled pools of the Beaverkill. I'd learned my knots. I tied my own leaders. I'd read my Bergman, my Flick, my Charles Meck, my Lefty Kreh. I'd paid my dues—sleeping in cars, living for days at a time on convenience-store pizza and potato chips, fishing hung over, fishing mud-brown rivers in the pouring rain, taking dunkings, spending endless hours on buses, being hazed by Jim Deren, losing favorite hats and sunglasses to the rivers, having my tackle box stolen. I'd even dreamed about rivers and angling, if that counts for anything, and had walked the streets of New York and ridden the subways absorbed in thought about them, as distracted as any scholar pondering a parable in the Kabbalah.

I liked to think that I had ten or eleven seasons "under my belt." But when you really think about it, what the hell does that mean? One fly fisherman's season, if he lives far from a river but is reasonably lucky, might consist of only a dozen or fifteen outings, while a much more serious and better-situated angler's might consist of ten times as many. Or, put another way: When the first angler tells you he has been fly fishing for ten years, he is referring to the equivalent of but one year for the second angler. Comparatively, he's hardly been fishing at all. Which means that these references to experience so casually and often boastfully thrown around don't necessarily mean much.

At any rate, the East Branch rather quickly disabused me, that first season, of any notion that I had already become a highly competent fly fisherman. It exposed all my many shortcomings. This was harder, leaner fishing than I was accustomed to, requiring a more knowledge-able, more versatile, more well-rounded angler than I was at the time—at least, if one wanted to catch the better trout in the river.

For example, the East Branch made me realize how badly I was handicapping myself by my dislike of fishing streamers and my even stronger dislike of fishing nymphs down deep, with weight (since overcome, as noted earlier, but at the time: too clunky, too laborious, and all those snags—forget it). I certainly was no dry-fly purist, since I was willing to use traditional wet flies—very traditional, as in Gold-Ribbed Hare's Ear, Leadwing Coachman, and Royal Coachman—and unweighted nymphs when the dries weren't working. But you might say I was a dry-fly/wet-fly purist, and as a consequence I generally denied myself access to the lower levels of the trout's world—where, in fact, the best fish spend most of their time.

The East Branch also made me aware of how much time I often wasted blithely casting all over the place rather than purposefully seeking out and focusing on the best holding water. (I think I was just as intent sometimes on making my dry fly land exactly where I wanted it to as on having a fish eat it.) It made me see how as a confirmed pre-sentationist, I had allowed myself to become incurious about all but the main hatches, a type of willful ignorance (don't give me the Latin, give me an Adams!). It made me realize how my neglect of using a stream thermometer to get a better idea how the trout were behaving was hurting my cause—as if I could somehow just dope these things out. How dopey was that?

Just as important as anything else, the East Branch opened my eyes to the large, self-defeating stubbornness that too often marked my fishing. Occasionally this stubbornness worked for me, but far more often it worked against. It was most apparent in my perverse refusal to give up on an unproductive piece of water and move on, as if it were personal and I could will a trout to take my fly and was sure to prevail if I stuck it out. Which, of course, was rarely the case.

I think I know how this bad habit began. One day very early in my fly-fishing life, I was fishing the Willowemoc in a heavy rain. The water was a sickly brown and rising fast. Since I wasn't catching anything anyway, I decided just to cast my Muddler Minnow to the exact same spot next to the bank for as long as I could stand it. It was a great-looking spot, about the size of a bathtub, one of those deep, slack-water havens scooped out of the bank where you know a good trout could be, so favorable is it to a satisfying life of bug eating and cannibalism. Making short casts, always to the same point at the top of the tub, I plopped the Muddler down, let it drift the length of the tub, and repeated. I lost count of my casts somewhere in the twenties but kept at it.

Finally came the cast when the moment the Muddler touched down, it was annihilated by a fourteen-inch brown trout that came halfway out of the water and set the hook without my help. It seemed clear to me that the trout struck the fly not because it wanted to eat it, but because it was sick and tired of seeing the stupid thing plop down up there and just wanted to kill it. That was one angry trout. Ever since that experience I had all too often fallen under the spell of a little incantation between my ears: *Just one more cast . . . you never know . . . one more . . . one more. . . .*

Discovering how much I still had to learn as an angler was a direct consequence of my now being able to fish all the time instead of only on irregular, often well-spaced trips. Deficiencies are easy to overlook if you're not doing something—fly fishing, fly tying, cooking, playing an instrument, quilting, chess, anything—constantly, day after day. By spending far more hours on the water than I ever had, and on fairly stingy water at that, I was repeatedly seeing what an "incompleat" angler I still was. Not by any stretch a novice, to be sure, but still sort of an intermediate, on a good day a high intermediate, on a bad day not so high, autodidactically groping my way along.

Actually, the best fishing I had that first full season was not on the East Branch but on Dry Brook in Arkville—the same stretch of water that John Burroughs traveled at the start of his journey down the East Branch more than a hundred years earlier. Though not remotely as attractive as the East Branch, this water became kind of a companion stream to me because it was a very short drive from my cabin, thus quick to reach when there was little daylight left or time was otherwise short, and was easy to enter from the bridge passing over it on Route 28. Also, I often caught more and better fish there. I suspect this was because the water was generally colder, being fed as it was by water coming down from forest tributaries like Rider Hollow—where the young A.J. McClane hid his brook-trout skillet. The setting was far from sylvan—often I'd be fishing within shouting distance of the Route 28 traffic and a small trailer park—but the stream itself would have been ideal if situated deep in the forest, and I was glad to have it.

Numerous times that spring, especially in June, this section of Dry Brook proved useful after a poor outing on the East Branch left me needing an ego boost. Often I could find a few strong, eager brownies there of eleven to thirteen inches, even bigger, that would rise to a cream or yellow dry fly, size 14 or 16, or pounce on a wet fly, or on a dry fished wet, and then give everything they had in fight. It was smaller water than the East Branch but just as rich in insect life: light-bodied mayflies in many sizes; small yellow and lime-green stone flies; big golden stone flies; multitudinous caddis flies; slate drakes, the nymphs of which, still wet, clung to the stones they had climbed onto at the edge of the stream; and more. There were times when it was not darkness that forced me to leave this water but the extraordinary number of feasting bats.

Today, this part of Dry Brook is different from what it was then, a section of it having been lined with riprap after epic flooding caused by Hurricane Irene in 2011.

———

That summer was very hot and dry, a bad one for trout fishing. Dog-day conditions started early: By July 1 the upper East Branch and all freestone streams were extremely low, more like the way we expect to see them in mid-August. A few months later Judy Van Put, in her "Hook, Line & Sinker" column in the *Catskill Mountain News*, wrote that "the summer of 1991 will be remembered as one of the hottest and driest in many years. Old-time anglers report never to have seen streams so low and warm, for such a long period throughout the summer, with generally poor stream fishing being found everywhere." Knowing of course that trout are stressed by warm water and can easily die in such conditions after going through the struggle of being caught and released, I spent painfully little time on the East Branch that July and August.

But as hard as the great heat and the dry air were on the rivers and my fishing, they were glorious up on my hemlock-shaded mountainside, where memories of the past winter still lingered in my bones. Warmth and comfort twenty-four/seven—exquisite. The heat baked wonderful cedar and tar smells out of the cabin. The insects sang ecstatically. After a few months of attentive grass cutting with the power mower that came with the place, I decided to let the grass and the weeds grow free and the yard return to meadow. My little one-acre plot turned out to be a regular raspberry farm, and I spent almost as much time gathering and eating wild raspberries as I did fishing, or trying to fish. I quit smoking for five and a half days and during that time had a dream in which my chest started rumbling and quaking and then split open and a huge snake, enraged, came squirming out.

If you did want to fish the upper East Branch that summer, the best time was right at the break of dawn, when the water was coolest and most oxygenated and the trout, if you could find them, were most likely to be feeding and least likely to be fatally exhausted after being caught and released.

The second-best time was at the other end of the night, after the sun had set and darkness was coming on, cooling the water. That was when I went out. I didn't have much choice, really. Nature or habit or both, I don't know which—all those years working late into the night on newspapers, perhaps—had calibrated my inner clock to make me wide awake late at night and well into the wee hours of the morning. Daybreak fishing is beautiful and productive, but it's awfully hard to do with any regularity on two or three hours' sleep. As a younger man, I did it all the time—I thought nothing of going fishing at dawn even on no sleep—but once I was living in Margaretville, it wasn't necessary. I lived on a river now; I didn't have to suffer to get my angling in. So I was (and continue to be) mainly an afternoon-and-evening fisherman.

It tickled me to learn that the revered Theodore Gordon, who was undoubtedly as committed to fly fishing, as engrossed in it, as anyone who ever lived, himself preferred to stay in bed rather than be astream at sunup. "I have heard that between dawn and sunrise was the best hours for a jumbo trout," he wrote in 1908 in *Forest and Stream*, an American outdoor magazine to which he contributed. "I have always intended to try this recipe, but never did. It involves getting up in the middle of the night, and a long tramp on an empty stomach." Thus spaketh St. Theodore.

My occasional late-evening outings on the East Branch during that long summer of drought never amounted to much. Sometimes I'd catch a small brown trout or two, hauling them in and releasing them as quickly as possible. More often I'd catch chubs, some of them surprisingly big. But at least I'd hear the trickling of the water and feel the stored-up heat of the stones and smell the sweetly dank, sour smell of the jungly summertime grasses and weeds and get my little fix of the river, enough to carry me through.

Mentioning Gordon just now reminds me of something else from that summer that, while it lasted only seconds and was in most respects unremarkable, clearly was of major importance to me, since it was burned into my angler's brain and gleams as brightly there now as it did then.

It was an afternoon in the last week of August. The heat had let up, and a lot of recent rain had lifted the streams. I had already seen that first patch of yellow high up on Pakatakan Mountain that so furtively signaled the imminence of fall and, shortly thereafter, winter. On the way to my Saturday-night job at the Emory Brook in Fleischmanns, I pulled over on Route 28 east of Arkville to steal an hour's fishing, or at least casting, on the Bush Kill, which there runs along 28 at the bottom of a wooded bank. As always, my Fisher glass rod was in my little Mazda GLC Sport (thirdhand), assembled and ready to go, the Light Cahill I'd been using my last time out still attached to the tippet.

It's a rather steep drop from the road down to the stream, and except in the winter months, when the bare trees allow greater visibility, it's easy not even to know there's a stream there. The bank is one of those unfortunate places that seem irresistible to the sort of people who throw beer cans and black plastic trash bags containing God knows what out car windows, but once you're down on the stream, it's quite nice. It's small water, but plenty big enough for trout to be able to live long and dine well. The first time I'd gone to that part of the Bush Kill, the previous May, the bottom was covered with caddis casings as dense and crunchy as gravel, and at one point, after I'd stood in the same spot a long while, a plump trout of twelve or thirteen inches glided slowly past me on its way upstream. I saw this as a come-on and vowed to return.

The day was spectacularly sunny and bright, not a cloud in view, a glorious day for being outdoors if not for good fly fishing. Approaching a trout stream without being seen by the fish is hard enough on level ground in low light, but coming down a bank in bright sunlight is that much harder, and I took great pains to move slowly and quietly and to stay low and hidden. I was moving in a downstream direction so as to be able to fish upstream into the best-looking water, staying as far back from the stream as the bank would allow and using all the cover available to me.

But I didn't pull it off. Something I did wrong, some small move I made, gave me away. As I was looking at the water, there was suddenly a burst, a frenzy, of small trout that I hadn't even seen. They were in a panic, darting around wildly in the sun-filled water. Then, just as quickly, they were gone, as were whatever chances I might have had of catching one of the better trout that had no doubt witnessed the panic from their lairs and were now on high alert. Small or large, trout see everything.

I leaned my rod against a tree, sat down, and stared at the empty water. This fly-fishing game could trip you up in so many different ways. I thought of Ray Bergman, who in *Trout* demonstrates time and again his absolute commitment to making whatever efforts are required, no matter how uncomfortable or time-consuming, to remain unnoticed by fish. In contrast to the sorry amateur performance I'd just given, he takes a half hour if necessary just to wade into position to cast, and then waits another half hour before casting, just to make sure the trout aren't spooked. He thinks nothing of approaching a pool by wading on his knees, or of casting, however awkwardly and uncomfortably, while lying hidden in tall grass on the bank. Would I ever achieve the same extraordinary level of discipline and patience?

If there is one lesson a trout fisherman can never learn and relearn too many times, it is this ridiculously self-evident but wickedly difficult one of staying invisible, and in all ways undetectable, to the fish. It pains me to think of how many times I must have unknowingly sent every fish in the neighborhood into hiding before even starting to cast, and then blamed something else for my lack of success. Like Bergman, Theodore Gordon was acutely aware of how easily and often anglers do this, and refers to it several times in his writings. "The great desideratum in fly-fishing is to keep out of sight of the keen eyes of the trout," he said in *Forest and Stream*. "Beware also of casting the shadow of your person or of your moving rod over the water you are about to fish."

I've never forgotten that tempest of little trout in the luminous afternoon water of the Bush Kill, over so fast but etched into memory for all my angling life. To this day I think I see it at least once every time I go fishing.

❧

One day late that fall, after all the leaves had come down and the first light snow had dusted the highest reaches of Pakatakan Mountain, and I had sealed all the windows with clear plastic again and hung the heavy quilt in the doorway between the kitchen and the living room, I was hitchhiking west on Route 28 toward Margaretville—I forget what was wrong with my car—when an elderly man picked me up. He asked me if I was a native of the area or a flatlander, and then said he had moved there from somewhere near New York City after retiring.

"The first two winters," he said, "I went so crazy from boredom I almost drank myself to death. I wasn't even a drinker, but here I was drinking so much I wound up in the hospital. Now I've adjusted. I've gotten used to it. But it was rough, let me tell you."

CHAPTER FIVE

Hermitry 101—Cabin fever—
My greatest fishing experience—
So much to know—Flirting with absurdity

I DIDN'T STRAY FAR FROM MY MOUNTAINSIDE THAT WINTER. I'D leave it to go to one of my highly part-time jobs, or to walk into the village to go to the A&P or the library. Sometimes, if the roads were free of ice, I'd bundle up extra heavily and ride my old Panasonic bicycle instead of walking. But for the most part I was content just to hole up with my fires, my radio, my dartboard, my electric typewriter, my reading—that was the winter I finally read (or, perhaps more accurately, overcame) *The Compleat Angler*, by Izaak Walton—my coffee, my whiskey, my beer, and my fishing tackle. I was a simple man growing simpler. ("Who the hell are you?" lamented a woman I had sort of liked when she saw the meager appointments of my TV-less life.)

By now I had become more or less a connoisseur of winter temperatures, and constantly kept an eye on my indoor and outdoor thermometers so as to keep up with whatever adjustments I had to make to stay comfortable. Which, with my fires and small electric heater and carefully rationed propane, I did. In my long johns and layered clothing and knit cap, I felt just fine even in a living-room temperature in the mid-fifties, though I would crank it up for company.

Except for my only full-time neighbor, Bill, whom most days I didn't see, there was no one else around. I liked the silence, the stillness, the sounds of my feet crunching in the snow and my maul

93

splitting the maple, oak, and birch for big aromatic fires at night that flamed so hot they made me sweat. I liked the low winter sky as evening came on, the transcendent delicacy of its icy blues, grays, violets, pinks, and yellows; and the snowfields at night when the moon was so bright there was a hint of blue in the dark sky and I cast a shadow on the snow two people could easily have tossed a ball around. In the deepest, darkest, coldest part of the winter, when the winds whistled and the snow hit my face like sand, time itself seemed to ice over, to slow almost to a stop, and I had an accruing hallucinatory sense that summer was a season that existed only in the imagination, in dreams.

Sometimes I walked down the hill to the Red Barrel. There I could sit in a booth by the window and drink coffee and read the *Oneonta Daily Star* and the *Kingston Daily Freeman*, and listen to people talk.

"It ain't this windy up home."

"You shoulda seen how he drug her away from the bar."

"I saw that big maple log comin' down the hill at me, I warmed up real fast!"

"She's pretty run down. She just lost her mom. She only lost her father last year. And her daughter was in a wreck up Highmount and was hurt pretty bad. Comin' over the hill there."

"You just sort of swallow and go on."

I'd watch out the window as people pulled up to and away from the gas pumps in their cars and pickups. GOD, GUNS AND GUTS MADE AMERICA, a bumper sticker said. LET'S KEEP ALL THREE. Since snow, ice, rain, and road salt are abundant in the Catskills and personal income often small, far more of the vehicles were rust buckets than in more prosperous areas downstate. Several local pickup trucks, or at least parts of them, were actually being held together with duct tape, which anyone who's been poor and has had to make things last knows is just about as important to living as bread and milk. Some of the working guys pulling up to the Red Barrel pumps were also using it as patch material on their heavy winter coveralls. Eventually, in my last fishing season in Margaretville, I'd be using it to hold the reel seat together on my fly rod.

There were moments that winter when my obvious taste and capacity for this sort of life—the solitude, the silence, the minimal human interaction—alarmed me a little. Just a little, in the way of causing a nervous laugh now and then. I believed it was a blessing of nature and disposition, a gift, to be able to be so content, even happy, being by oneself a lot. But I also sensed that if I wasn't careful, the blessing could gradually be distorted into a curse. As much as I loved solitude and silence, as much as I missed them when I didn't have them, as perfect from start to finish as I regarded many of those frigid, snowy, people-less winter days in and around my cabin, as indisputably as the call to isolation pulsed deep inside me, I absolutely did not want to become a full-fledged recluse, the increasingly odd dropout from all the hurts and complications and challenges of life, living alone in a shack up in the hemlock trees on the mountainside, seen from time to time walking along Route 28 or eccentrically riding a bicycle even in winter, talking to no one, not participating even minimally; perhaps, in time, not even opening the front door if someone besides the Jehovah's Witnesses were bold enough or curious enough to knock on it. I was living sort of an introductory version of that life—Hermitry 101—and I liked it. Oh yes, I liked it. I was acing it. But I didn't want to become *that person*, and I was old enough, experienced enough, to know how insidiously these things happen. One day a man or a woman thinks, *How did I get to be this? What went wrong? I thought I was paying attention!*

Clearly, though, I was willing to play with the idea.

❦

Then came the big day, March 1, with its promise of joyful liberation from the long deep freeze. Unfortunately, that particular March brought no such relief, few if any of the sweet signs of imminent spring that March usually brings and that are so important to people's psyches in upstate New York. Deep into the month, day after day was cold, gray, raw, sullen, the sky an unrelenting gloom. The sun became a distant memory; the brown hills were like heaps of rusting scrap metal; the snow just kept falling. In the third week of the month, when spring officially began, it got extremely cold and the water main froze up where it entered the cabin, which was starting to feel like a tomb.

One day I realized that I'd become more or less constantly sad, impatient, and pissed off at everything. The diagnosis was easy: cabin fever. I had managed to escape this affliction my first winter in the cabin, but now, thanks to this bleak, frigid, interminable March, it had me. I was going a little crazy, but at least I knew it. I read with new interest the police-blotter accounts in the local newspapers of domestic disputes, public altercations, public intoxication, DWI arrests, guys getting boozed up and tormenting their estranged wives or ex-girlfriends, and so on. Every time I read these brief accounts of people bollixing up their lives, or being bollixed up by them, I also read, or at least imagined, a subtext: *I've had enough! The cold! The snow! The gray and brown! The bare trees as good as dead! The plastic on the windows! The propane bills! The stinky long johns! You! Me! This place! I need light and warmth! I at least gotta get drunk!*

My neighbor Bill had had enough, too. One afternoon late that month, I was walking up the dirt road as yet another new snow was falling. I was on my way into the state forest, where I loved to be and to tramp when heavy snow was coming down through the trees; it was a little like church, but quieter, holier, and cheaper. Bill was standing in his doorway in his undershirt, looking out at the snow, up at the sky, with disgust. "When the hell is this gonna stop?" he called out.

He invited me in for a beer, and Bill and I spent the rest of the afternoon sitting at his kitchen table watching the snow come down and drinking Milwaukee's Best. Bill said he was disturbed by the amount of beer he'd been drinking lately (I'd been knocking back a fair amount of Genesee Cream Ale myself). "Nineteen cans yesterday," he said. "Nineteen cans! Nineteen!" A couple of times he hinted that he'd fallen down on the floor once or twice. Then he said very forcefully that he expected to be found dead one day on his cabin floor. "Right there, Mitch," he said, pointing with his cigarette to a spot on the floor not far from the table. "That's where they're gonna find me. Right there."

———————

For a certain privileged minority of those who do it, fly fishing is a pretty fancy enterprise, pursued globally. Ask some anglers you see browsing in a New York City fly shop to name the high point of their fishing lives, and the chances are good that at least one of them will mention a trip to some exotic locale like Argentina or New Zealand or the Kamchatka Peninsula in Russia, or Iceland or Norway, or even Mongolia or the Amazon. The once huge world has shrunk, and there are landing strips, guides, and single malt everywhere. All it takes is dough.

Other fishermen, probably of more modest means, may cite that one joyous trip they've managed to take so far to the Yellowstone region of Wyoming, Montana, and Idaho. Others may tell the story of the best fish they ever hooked into, whether they landed it or not. There are fish whose weight and strength we never forget even if we lost them, even if we never got a glimpse of them. They live on in our imaginations long after they've died a natural death or been eaten by a bear or sizzled to a tasty crisp in a bait fisherman's oven.

In naming the high point of my own angling life so far, I don't have to consider a single fishing trip outside North America, because as of this writing, there haven't been any. I've taken many trips to the American West, and a few of them, or things that happened on them, would be contenders.

But it's really no contest. The experience that keeps coming to mind over all the others occurred in my second full season on the East Branch, when over one period of almost four weeks—twenty-six straight days, to be exact, covering almost all of June and spilling over into July—I fished every single day and came as close as I ever have or probably ever will to a continuous, twenty-four/seven immersion in the life, the self-contained parallel reality, of fly fishing for trout.

Now, I've never actually aspired, not seriously, to escape so-called real life, whether through the stupefaction of booze or drugs or, for that matter, the high of fly fishing; and at any rate, rivers and fish and angling *are* real life. But I think those twenty-six days were as close to true escape from the everyday world as I've ever come, a kind of gradual, luxurious drifting away into a rare state of sustained contentment. They were probably the fullest realization of my desire to live on a trout river in the first place—twenty-six straight days when life was stripped down to the river, the fish, the bugs, the woods, the rocks, the sun, the sky, the moon, the rain, the breeze, the casting of my rod, the clicking of my reel, and no question more pressing, day after day, than where to fish and which fly to use.

This was life. Everything else was just a distraction. Even sustenance consisted primarily of hot dogs, potato chips, and coffee grabbed at the Sunoco station convenience store on Main Street on my way to the river. (Fly fishermen can go for weeks on hot dogs, potato chips, and coffee, especially with an occasional chocolate bar or Twinkie thrown in.) Fishing owned my days, my thoughts, my senses. Even when I wasn't doing it, I was occupied with it in one way or another:

making leaders, casting in the yard, cleaning my Cortland peach double-taper line, reading up on bugs and techniques, in general getting ready for that day's trip to the stream. Late nights usually found me, just in from the river, sitting at my desk examining captured duns and spinners in the lamplight. I went to bed thinking about the river and the trout and woke up thinking about them. My main retreat into the regular world was when I went to my Saturday-night dishwashing job to make a few bucks and have a real meal and a glass or two of wine with my friends there.

It helped that during this twenty-six-day period, the highly variable Catskill weather was consistently good and often beautiful. There were evenings on the East Branch of such visual perfection, with the famous Catskill mists gathering over the water and the moon rising from the woolly green hills up into the limpid, glittery sky, and the deer sipping at the edge of the stream and maybe even a leaping trout or two, that it all looked ridiculously like the infantile depictions of paradise often seen on the covers of religious pamphlets. Sometimes I had to sit down on the bank or a fallen tree and just take it in. I knew, of course, that behind the arcadian scenes coyotes were disemboweling fawns; grownup trout were eating baby trout; eagles and hawks were murdering furry little mammals and invading the nests of weaker birds to kill and eat all the occupants; shrews were killing and eating mice; snakes were swallowing other animals alive; and the enormous snapping turtle I saw from time to time—it drifted past me in the current once, just a few feet away, underwater—had dismembered and chomped to death countless frogs, crayfish, and ducklings. It was a slaughterhouse out there, but it sure was lovely to behold.

Some people may be surprised to learn that during this experience that I call the most memorable of my angling life, the fishing itself, though better than the previous year, was rather ordinary. But lengths, weights, and fish counts were not the point. I was living my version of the angling life to the max, freer from nonangling distractions and intrusions than I ever had been and possibly ever would be again. That was the point. Most outings I caught at least one or two respectable trout; several times I got skunked; and as often as I got skunked I caught up to a half-dozen beefy, jumping battlers of, say, ten to thirteen inches, maybe two or three of fourteen. I'm sure I didn't catch anything bigger during those twenty-six days. It was also during this period that, for the first time, I caught a couple of rainbow trout in the upper East Branch, in addition to all the browns. One afternoon I drove across the mountains to fish the water on the upper Beaverkill that I had fished so often in years past, and there I took four surprisingly good brook trout. They were hanging out in deep, well-shaded, well-oxygenated water next to a bank, and energetically attacked a McMurray Ant, an Isonychia Nymph, and a Light Cahill dry.

So, nothing for the record books, but there you have it, and anyone who scoffs at having a muscular, unruly, indefatigable eleven-inch trout on the end of a 6X tippet doesn't get it anyway.

Sometimes I was dazed by the abundance and variety of the aquatic insect life on the East Branch. There were evenings that offered up such a mesmerizing jumble of mayflies, caddis flies, and stone flies in different colors, sizes, and stages of life that it was impossible for me to identify many or most of them with certainty. Even among some of the flies I felt confident identifying, there had long seemed to my inexpert eyes to be confusing variations, mostly in hue of body color, from one stream to the next. But were they just variations, or different flies altogether? I had also formed an unscientific impression that there were sporadic, low-density naturals that trout ate routinely but that were not in the books and that nobody seemed to know much about; and also that there were mayflies that seemed not to belong to any particular population but to be virtual solitaries, with no siblings, no fellows, just rising from the water and flying for the trees all by themselves, as if trying to slip through unseen.

There were many nights when I'd come home from the East Branch with a captured mayfly dun or spinner, get out my fishing books, examine the fly studiously under the desk lamp, compare it with the color photos and the drawings and the written descriptions in the books, and end up concluding—most unhappily—that it didn't convincingly match *any* of the examples in the books. Like many fly fishers, I suspect, I often had a feeling that my entomological knowledge was woefully inadequate, and that rank laziness or some other character flaw was preventing me from doing something about it. I knew I had a great deal to learn about the naturals. Of course, my firm belief that presentation trumped imitation was a deterrent of sorts to my learning it.

Similarly, I was very disappointed at times by my inability to figure out why the trout behaved as they did, especially when they didn't appear to be behaving at all—when they had shut down so completely that there didn't seem to be a single fish in the river. All fly fishermen of any experience have encountered this. Short of torrential rain, it is the worst sort of bad luck to have on that big day astream you've been looking forward to for months. The fish are there and you know they're there, even though they won't show themselves or give you the merest sign they're there, not even the slightest, most apathetic, most infrequent little bump of your fastidiously fished flies. They're in coma mode, and you're not going to catch them no matter what you do, excepting dynamite. These are the times that remind us that all our hard-acquired skills and knowledge don't add up to diddly-squat unless and until our primitive, pebble-brained adversaries are good and ready to humor us.

It didn't bother me that I couldn't catch fish when this was happening; what bothered me was that I didn't always know *why* it was happening. Usually I could make a plausible, educated guess: Maybe the trout were adjusting to some abrupt change in the water temperature, for instance—water temperature explains so much of trout behavior—or maybe they had fed so well before I showed up that they'd sunk into a long, postprandial languor. My angling tomes weren't always helpful. What I really wanted was for Lefty Kreh to step out of the woods the way those old ballplayers emerged from the cornfield in *Field of Dreams*, and give me the lowdown. I knew Lefty would know. As for the merely mortal authorities I had access to in real life—the guys who worked in fly shops, for example, or the fishermen who hung around in fly shops, eager to be consulted—I had already learned, many years earlier, that there was rarely unanimity or even consistency in their answers to my questions, though they usually tried their best and were honest about what they didn't know. Of course, this is one of the most seductive things about the whole obsessive enterprise: Nobody has ever figured it all out, and none of us is going to be the one who finally does. But we try to be anyway.

Toward the end of that fishing season, as the trees were shedding their leaves and the chill was starting to come up through the floor into my feet and legs again, I got myself a new weapon against the swiftly advancing cold: a kerosene heater. I forget where I picked it up—it wasn't new. But it threw off a great deal of cheap, powerful heat, and I could move it around from place to place. Kerosene became my main source of heat for that winter and the three more winters to come in the cabin.

In all other respects, though, the final months of the year were dismal. It was time to pony up for my summer of fly fishing—for my trancelike twenty-six straight days, my July and August afternoons and evenings so blessed that season with cool weather and full rivers, my September afternoons and evenings devoted to nothing more gainful than waving a fly rod back and forth amid storms of cinnamon caddis and trying to fool trout into eating my invariably insufficiently infinitesimal imitations of minute blue-winged olives.

It was time to pay the bill, but with what? Ah, the angling life. By now I no longer had even my Saturday-night job at the Emory Brook, having given it up to help my boyhood friend Bob move into a house in Cape Breton, Nova Scotia, and take my first crack at salmon fishing (hundreds of casts, no salmon). Once again I drove all over Delaware, Greene, and Ulster Counties, knocking on doors, filling out applications, looking for whatever work I could get. I knew from my lean years in the city that if I made enough calls and knocked on enough doors and kept coming back, eventually I'd land something. But it was much harder in the boonies, especially in the off-season. I'd drive through those little towns on Routes 28 and 30 and 23 and 23A on a cold, gusty November afternoon, and sometimes it seemed as if there weren't even any people in them, let alone jobs.

Having been shaped by a mother who lived through the Blitz and was the equal of Mrs. Miniver any day of the week, I've never shrunk from hardship. It would be like repudiating a heritage. But there were days during those dreary months when it all seemed absurd: the penury, the growling gut, the one-meal days, the long hours of searching for menial work, the gas gauge never far from empty, the stack of unpaid bills on the desk, the poor-man's plastic on the windows, the frozen pipes, the lying under the car all day in frigid weather to change the water pump or fix the brake lines or do whatever else was necessary to keep it limping along, the extravagance of buying a six-pack of beer, the snapping sound in the kitchen as another shrew bit the dust.

For what purpose? To what end? Just to be able to fish a lot from April to October? And to write what I wanted to write whether it made me any money or not? Just to be able to try, at least, to carry out some quixotic idea of a simple, truthful, crap-free life committed to and built around a small number of highly desirable things?

The days got shorter, darker, colder. There were mornings when I got out of bed with all the enthusiasm of a man going to work in the mines. Sometimes I thought of something that my friend Max, a poet and commercial fisherman on eastern Long Island, had said during a recent visit: that he had finally realized and accepted that "the way things are is the way they're always gonna be."

CHAPTER SIX

Ten thousand dollars!—Professional
advancement—Fly-fishing failure—
Bergman on my mind—The angler
I wanted to be—A legendary local

SEEK, AND YE SHALL FIND. EVENTUALLY THAT WINTER I WAS WORKING two kitchen jobs, one on Friday and Saturday nights at the Owl's Nest, a large family restaurant in Highmount, eight miles from my cabin; the other on Sunday nights at the Woodland Valley Inn, a much smaller restaurant in Phoenicia, about twenty miles down Route 28. Combining this employment with whatever odd jobs I was able to get here and there, I was slipping by. It looked as if I'd be able to make it to another fishing season without going under.

Given all the usual snow and ice and the fact that I could never be sure something wouldn't go wrong with my entirely self-repaired, self-maintained car, getting to and from my Phoenicia job always had a feeling of expeditionary adventure. This was particularly true of the trip home, which I made at an hour when Route 28 had become largely empty of traffic, of human life. Although my car never failed me on these trips, one Sunday it wouldn't start because of a frozen gas line and I had to hitchhike to Phoenicia. I got there in time, but my attempt to hitch home five or six hours later was futile. The blacktop was a long, dark, frozen emptiness, and the drivers of the few vehicles that did come along chose prudence over charity, for which I couldn't blame them.

I ended up walking all the way home, exactly 20.6 miles—I measured it on the odometer the next time I drove. For anyone wondering how long it takes to walk 20.6 miles over hilly terrain in heavy work boots in single-digit temperatures, the answer is seven hours, forty minutes. The blisters slow you down.

One night in the Woodland Valley kitchen, there was a moment that made such an impression on me that I thought about it for years afterward and sometimes still do. Our chef had recently been fired— I doubt that any business has turnover like the restaurant business, which in certain respects is much like the old-time, long-gone newspaper business, when newsrooms provided gainful refuge for all sorts of dropouts, malcontents, soreheads, authority haters, smart-asses, alcoholics, potheads, hotheads, and congenital trash-basket kickers. The fired chef's replacement, Chaz, a tall, strapping young guy with blond hair, probably not yet thirty, was telling us how he'd been working hard and saving his money and was planning to take a ski vacation in the Rocky Mountains.

Then he said—not boasting, just matter-of-factly—that he had managed to put away ten thousand dollars in the bank. I was astounded. He might as well have said ten million dollars. I could barely conceive of having so much money, of how completely different my life would be if I had ten thousand dollars. I wondered, as I worked there at the dishwashing machine in my corner of the room, the lowest, most pitiful person in the social order of the kitchen, virtually nonexistent to any waitress who might catch my eye, what it must be like to wake up in the morning knowing you've got ten thousand dollars in the bank and can pay all your bills and, oh my God, travel across the country in pursuit of recreation.

I thought of all the things I could do if I had ten thousand dollars: Pay up my account with the fuel company and have them fill the propane tank again. Pay off my credit-card balance—it sure would shock those folks to see something more than the minimum payment for a change! Get health insurance. Go to a dentist for that tooth that was starting to bother me. Treat myself to a new fly rod, a graphite—Del-Sports in Margaretville had Cortlands for under a hundred bucks. Get a new thirdhand car. Take a trip to Montana!

Years later, when I was back in the world of full-time employment and the day finally came when I saw that I had ten thousand dollars, I thought right away of Chaz and his gobsmacking utterance that night in the kitchen of the Woodland Valley Inn, and it pleased me immensely to know that I was now in the same exalted company.

I quit my job at the Woodland Valley when the owner of the Owl's Nest, where I was already working Fridays and Saturdays, offered me Sundays, too. Since he paid six dollars an hour to the Woodland Valley's five, it was an offer I had to take. Better yet, I didn't have to run the dishwashing machine very long before one of the two line cooks abruptly quit and I was put into training to replace him. In no time at all, I was a cook, a huge upward move professionally and socially if not so much financially. I was tempted to go down to the Woodland Valley on a night off just to sit at the bar and show how far I'd come in the world, but I refrained.

I was in charge of all the fish and pasta. My fellow line cook and immediate boss, Jim, was in charge of all the meat dishes and the soups and ran the kitchen. I made baked salmon, salmon and sole *al cartoccio*, shrimp scampi, and various linguine dishes. A few hours before opening, I chopped and sliced vegetables for the salad bar and made the coleslaw. I was actually learning things on this job, such as how to chop and slice vegetables properly and quickly, and how to make a roux, that would serve me well for the rest of my life. I was also consuming so much food by nibbling—french fries, cheese, shrimp, linguine—that for the first time ever, I started to grow a modest paunch. "What's that?" a waitress said one day, pointing at it. I can heartily advise any poor person looking for a basic job to get one in a restaurant kitchen. At least you will eat.

We were all doing our prep one afternoon when a young waitress, not long out of high school, started telling me about her financial problems. She said she was already scarily in debt because she couldn't make payments on her credit cards and an auto loan. She said her boyfriend was partly to blame because he had abused her credit cards when she'd let him use them. Nevertheless, she had just given him a gift of a new gun rack, which cost her a couple of hundred dollars, because she was tired of seeing all his rifles every time she opened the closet door. Since the new gun rack held twelve rifles, this would not be an issue anymore, which delighted her. She was angry with her boyfriend for abusing her credit cards but retained faith in him. "He can change," she said.

—◆—

One evening in early June, I was fishing the East Branch not far from the Old Stone Schoolhouse, a one-room structure two miles from town that was built in 1820, rebuilt in 1860, and served Margaretville as a school, a social center, and even a church for well more than a century.

Since arriving at the stream around six thirty, I had seen—or believed I had, allowing for both my fallibility in insect identification and the steadily fading light—little sulphurs; big sulphurs; blue-winged olives; Light Cahill-type duns and spinners (using that designation, Light Cahill, rather loosely); a couple of March brown (or gray fox) duns and maybe some spinners; maybe some slate drakes, aka mahogany duns (*Isonychia bicolor*); several kinds of caddis, including cinnamons and dark blue sedges; a few small and tiny duns whose identities I could not even guess; and clouds of similarly unidentifiable spinners.

Now, in the last half hour or so of daylight, the air was filled with mayflies going through their beautiful twilight pageant of life and death. To my left, to my right, in the water ahead of me and the water behind, trout were feeding. It was the sort of late-spring evening that a Catskill fly fisherman lives for.

But I wasn't able to get a single trout to take one of my dry flies. I had plenty of rises, but they were all rejections, and finally I was reduced to that repetitive, hasty, desperate sort of fly changing that is the last resort of the defeated angler. Then it was too dark to continue. I had to quit and wade back to the bank, and accept the bitter fact that I had bungled the opportunity that the river, the flies, and the trout had so opulently given me that fine June evening. I did my best to take it in stride, but it was hard.

As I often did in those days when I felt I had fished poorly (or, for that matter, well), I thought of the scene in Ray Bergman's *Trout*, one of my favorite in all fishing writing, in which Bergman, hidden "under heavy foliage" on the bank of a river overlooking a pool, carefully observes and judges the anglers who, one after another, appear at the bottom of the pool and fish their way through it. I have covertly watched other fly fishermen at work myself, many times, hoping to learn a thing or two. Sometimes I've gone away instructed and enlightened, other times with a stupidly smug sense of superiority that lasts only until the next time I snag my backcast in a tree or stumble on a stone and send every trout in the river into hiding. In other words, not long.

But imagine it: fishing innocently, unknowingly, under the clinical gaze of one of the great American masters, every move you make being analyzed and judged. Of the ten fishermen Bergman watches over "a half day," only one cuts it as the real deal. "I almost shouted with admiration," he writes. "Here was a real angler and no mistake."

I wondered what Ray would have thought if he'd sat hidden in the foliage along the East Branch that night and watched the angler at work there. I asked myself the question but didn't want to think of the answer. There was so far to go yet from where I was to where I wanted to be.

⬩

That spring, snow had lingered high up on Belleayre Mountain, site of a popular ski area, until late May. The final thaw and melt was long and slow, the rivers that April so high that real fishing was all but impossible until the month had ended. But fishing conditions can change abruptly in the Catskills: By early July it was extremely hot and the upper East Branch was rapidly dropping, drying up, shriveling away. It looked as if we were in for a repeat of the drought of '91.

At first, just as I had during that summer two years earlier, I limited myself to sporadic outings only in the last hour or hour and a half of daylight, when I hoped to find that the water had cooled to an ethically fishable temperature, the maximum of which by my lights was sixty-nine. The fishing was predictably bad, though, and soon I gave up on it altogether. I was starting to be a little too casual about the water temperature anyway, which gnawed at me. Mostly I caught chubs, which with the suckers now seemed to have the river to themselves. One evening that summer, when the water was at its lowest and most inert, I saw a sight I had never seen before and haven't seen since: a poolful of suckers feeding at the surface, sometimes jumping heavily, clumsily, right through it.

But even though fishing on the upper East Branch had once again come to an end until fall, I found this time that it was harder for me to stay off the river, even in those conditions. I *liked* being out there in the dog days, no matter that actual fishing was out of the question. I liked the peacefulness I found there on those slow, sleepy, sultry days of high summer, when the lush natural world, after three or four months of nonstop burgeoning and growth, seemed to have exhausted itself to the point of torpor. Also, having made a personal commitment to this river, I think I felt something like a responsibility to be there when it was at its worst. Being on a favorite trout stream when the water has dropped as low as it can go, reducing its exuberant early-season voice to scarcely audible trickles and murmurs, baring fields of river-bottom stones to the baking sun, revealing every nook and cranny of the logjams and streambed depressions and gouged-out banks where trout hide when the water's up, exposing the rarely seen debris washed downstream over the decades—a tractor tire from the 1950s, a cheap folding beach chair, a golf ball from someone's blown tee shot years ago on the links a few miles upriver—is sort of like seeing it naked and infirm. It's a type of intimacy.

So I decided that just because I couldn't fish didn't mean I couldn't go out there in my hip waders and get my little East Branch fix. It didn't mean I couldn't work on my casting and other skills and continue to observe the river up close. So each dog-day outing became, basically, an elaborate form of practice. I broke down every component of my game from the moment I got close to the stream to the moment I left it, evaluating every single thing I did: my approach, my reading of the water, my wading and stalking, my casting and mending, my fly placement, my pickups and retrieves, my movements along the bank, my playing and releasing of a captured fish (even if only a pretend trout in the form of a chub), my knot tying and tippet changing—all of it. It wasn't as good as real fishing, to say the least, but it did make the summer count for something. Some days I went home with the fine feeling that I had done everything right and was coming along as a real angler, others with the nagging thought that I was just a mediocrity who'd been happily deluding himself for years.

Looking back, I can see now that one of my purposes on those dog-day afternoons and evenings of not-really-fishing was to make myself into a particular type of angler, the type I wanted to be, and that my model for the type of angler I wanted to be was the angler Ray Bergman watched and admired from his bosky poolside hiding place in *Trout*. It had already been a dozen years since I'd read *Trout*, but clearly that one anecdote, that little riverine tableau, was etched deep in my fisherman's psyche. Bergman's delight when he finally sees "a real angler" is so palpable. To a serious fly fisherman, his account of this man as he approaches the pool from downstream, pauses well below it to study it, and proceeds to fish it, casting first from his knees so as not to alert the nearest trout to his presence, is kind of thrilling. The attentiveness, the patience, the caution, the carefully considered decisions, the economy and efficiency of movement, the sure knowledge of what he is doing and what he is about, the versatility of skills—all are evident in Bergman's description of this anonymous, unwittingly immortalized fisherman. We even feel we have learned something about his character: He is thoughtful, thorough, patient, a man who does things right. Next to him, the other nine anglers who work the pool, many or most of whom probably thought rather highly of themselves as fly fishermen, do not measure up. And the biggest difference is above the shoulders.

This was the kind of angler I aspired to be. I didn't care about being the guy who could double haul a hundred feet or who used the finest bamboo rods and Bogdan reels or who could afford to hire guides to take him on drift boats and put him over spectacular trout on the West Branch of the Delaware or the great rivers of the West. All those things were fine. But I wanted to be the guy who mastered the fundamentals of up-close wade fishing and knew how to dissect a complicated pool or other stretch of water and found the fish that other anglers missed, and who used his noggin as much as his shoulder muscles.

I think that some version of Bergman's "real angler" is also what I'm hoping to see when I surreptitiously watch other fly fishermen fish (an insider's game, for sure—about as interesting to nonanglers as watching a writer write). I'm always hoping to see a master at work, an angler who not only catches fish—obviously the most important consideration—but, in the process, does everything right and makes every move count and displays a certain elegance as DiMaggio did on the baseball field. I would gladly go down to the nearest crossroads and sell my soul to the devil for such artistry astream. The few times I've witnessed it, though, I have felt no envy, no dejection over my own deficiencies, just admiration and the pleasure of knowing that, at least for some, it is attainable.

A couple of times on those drought-season outings I entertained myself by playing a little game. I imagined that my fly-fishing skills were being scored by an Olympics-like panel of judges who were all esteemed anglers, people like, say, Joan Wulff, Joe Brooks (what did it matter if they were dead or alive?), George LaBranche, Joe Humphreys, and John Goddard. How would these great experts judge my abilities?

"Oh, my," I'd hear the TV announcer say, "very pretty the way he side-armed that Adams into the little pocket between those low-hanging hemlock boughs. Listen to the crowd. I think he just locked up a nine on short-distance casting."

"Might have been a ten," the other guy in the broadcast booth would say, "if he'd played the breeze a little better on that last roll cast."

"I've been watching Joan Wulff, Ken," the other guy would say, "and I think she definitely likes what she's seeing."

"Everybody knows how hard Keller has been working," Ken would say. "He's well known for his work ethic, and it seems to be paying off here today."

"It'd be nice to see him take home a medal. Maybe then he could get rid of those cheap boot-foot waders and buy himself a real pair."

"He's one shabby-looking angler, Tom, that's for sure."

That was the summer of my first and only attempt to fish in the dead of night. For years I'd heard and read stories of fishermen catching ancient trout of enormous size in the pitch black of the wee hours, when such trout were known to bestir their secretive, cautious, lazy selves to go looking for a meal or two, preferably substantial enough to fuel their long, heavy bodies: other fish, mice, frogs, crayfish, really big bugs all asquirm in the moonlight. Dainty little mayflies or caddis 'neath the sunny blue sky didn't often interest these whoppers; those days were long behind them. In some of my fishing books, there were photos of anglers posing with these nocturnal prowlers in harsh artificial flashbulb light, the solid blackness of the night framing the picture of the ecstatic fisherman and the hapless jumbo trout—always a brown.

But my one post-midnight outing on the East Branch was a dud. I didn't catch anything and didn't really care. It wasn't for me. I didn't like not being able to see the world around me, not to mention my line and fly and where my casts came down. I stuck it out for maybe an hour and a half, then went home to bed, telling myself I'd try it again sometime. But I never did.

All of which brings me to Niles Fairbairn, one of the Margaret-ville area's best-known residents back in the twentieth century. The name Fairbairn (FAIR-burn) is one of the oldest and most wide-spread in the area; you can hardly get through a busy day in Margaret-ville without encountering it one way or another. Niles, born in 1886 in the remote Dry Brook Valley, was a renowned trapper and hunter who, according to his obituary in 1965 in the *Catskill Mountain News*, cobbled together a living in the time-honored Catskill way: "painter, paperhanger, farmer in Dry Brook, logger, sawmill operator, cook in restaurants and boarding houses, camp caretaker."

But what made Niles Fairbairn a local folk hero were his remarkable gifts for taming and training seemingly uncontrollable wild animals, like porcupines and bobcats, and catching huge brown trout in the East Branch—often, apparently, in the dark of night. As Ed Van Put writes in *Trout Fishing in the Catskills*: "He had a reputation for catching brown trout more than 5 pounds, and it was claimed that he only fished on moonless nights, with a #6 black fly. In June 1950, the *Catskill Mountain News* reported that Niles caught fourteen trout that month between 16 and 24 1/2 inches, with the largest weighing 5 3/4 pounds!"

Exclamation marks have been cheapened by overuse in the age of social media, but that one suits.

In July 1935, Helen Keller, whose overcoming of blindness and deafness had won her international admiration, was staying in the Dry Brook Valley, and Niles Fairbairn was asked to introduce her to trout fishing. So Keller, Fairbairn, and a companion who could communicate with Keller hit the stream. First, the account in the *Catskill Mountain News* said, Fairbairn taught his student how to cast the rod. Then Keller proceeded to catch one little trout and two good ones, the first of which was "a large sized native" that "she landed . . . after a ten minute fight in the swift waters."

When the outing was over, Helen Keller told her companion to tell Fairbairn, "I had the thrill of my life." I don't know if she was telling the truth or just being polite, but as a fisherman who's had a few long fights in the swift waters myself, I think she might have been on the level.

CHAPTER SEVEN

Rolling my own—Thirty below—
The best time of year—The flies I tied—
Fly-fishing perfection—
Catch-and-release misgivings

For the longest time, tying my own flies was one of those things I was definitely going to get around to one year, like quitting smoking and reading *Middlemarch*. But I kept putting it off, and as the fishing seasons went by, my inability to make my own flies started to weigh on me. It became harder and harder to reconcile my self-image as a serious fly fisherman with such a conspicuous hole in my repertoire.

I mean, a real angler rolls his own, doesn't he? Or she? He doesn't have to, but he can. Think about it: For all their vast knowledge and experience, would figures like Ernest Schwiebert, Lee Wulff, and A.J. McClane have commanded the authority they did if they couldn't even make their own trout flies? Would we retain our faith in them as master anglers if, God forbid, we were to learn that they had to go to the store and buy someone else's? I rest my case.

The final nudge I needed to start tying flies came one day early that next winter. I ran into a rather cocky young guy I knew in passing who had only recently taken up fly fishing but spoke about it with that glib, instant-expert confidence that seems to characterize a small but consistent percentage of newcomers to the sport. Nobody knows more about fly fishing, and nobody ever has and nobody ever will, than a certain type of man who's been doing it for about a month. Once or twice I had listened politely as my newbie acquaintance held forth on some aspect of angling that he really knew very little about. It was annoying as hell, but it was also amusing to watch him hang himself. "It ain't what a man don't know that makes him a fool," Josh Billings said, "but what he does know that ain't so."

Well, on that winter day this fellow told me he'd been taking fly-tying lessons and would bestow a few of his creations upon me, presumably to enhance the quality of my fishing experience. "Yeah, I'm starting to tie some pretty nice flies," he said. "Working on some killer nymphs right now. I'll give you a few."

The truth is, I have much to thank that man for. The fact that he was tying his own flies and I wasn't was all the motivation I needed. I already owned a beginner's fly-tying kit but had only dabbled with it over the years, producing a few "flies" that looked as if a chimp had made them. Now I rooted it out of the closet and began learning for real—as always, for better or worse, teaching myself.

Practicing a little every day, I managed to start tying some flies, mostly dries, that were a full level or two above a chimp's, though perhaps not much more. Fortunately, making flies that catch a few fish does not require high expertise in fly tying. Making good flies does, and making great flies requires a total commitment to mastering the methods and materials of the craft. But self-taught amateurs like me can be thankful that even poor flies will often work. And when I discovered that spring that the ratty little fruits of my slow, halting labors at my beginner's vise would actually catch fish, it was like having a door flung open to a whole new dimension of fly fishing, yet another beautiful thing to become obsessed with and ruin my life over. Maybe I could barely pay the rent; maybe I drove a car that looked as if I'd salvaged it from a scrap heap; maybe I never got anything in the mail but shutoff notices and rejection slips. So what? I could tie a Pale Evening Dun and catch trout with it. Beat that!

In addition to tying flies and slinging salmon *al cartoccio* at the Owl's Nest, shoveling snow and fixing burst water pipes kept me busy that winter, which was the coldest, snowiest, nastiest yet. On a couple of mornings in January, just before daybreak, the thermometer outside my kitchen window neared thirty below. Ice appeared in the drain in the shower floor, moving up from below like a little glacier. More than five feet of snow fell that month, and I regularly climbed up on the cabin roof to shovel it off, to prevent a collapse. The village, a maze of plowed-up snowbanks, was to my eye the prettiest it ever looked. Water lines popped on me left and right that winter, but by then I was an old hand at fixing them, having laid up a supply of new copper pipe and fittings and equipped myself with a pipe cutter, solder, a propane torch, and all the other necessities.

On my frequent walks down the hill to hang out at the Red Barrel or to fill my five-gallon kerosene container at the store's pump, I started running into a man who introduced himself as Jerry. Jerry lived alone in a little house much closer to Route 28 and said he was ninety-one years old. He stood as straight as a two-by-four; had curious, searching blue eyes; and spoke with invigorating clarity and directness. Obviously he could take care of himself, but still I used to wonder sometimes, given all the headaches of the Catskill winter, why a man of ninety-one wouldn't want to live in milder, easier climes. Then one day Jerry told me that he'd been a carpenter elsewhere in the state before retiring and going to live in Florida for a number of years. As soon as his wife died, he moved back to the cold, the snow, the black ice, the face-scalding wind. "I couldn't stand it down there," he said.

Even more so than usual, the mud season that year, the transition from winter to spring, was exhilarating not just to see—watching that old, dirty, dreary sea of snow slowly melt away, knowing it would not be back anytime soon—but to hear. There was a constant sound of moving water, all day and all night long, even in sleep and dreams, as the snowmelt and ice melt and frequent rain poured down the channels that countless past thaws had carved out of the mountainside and raced through the creek beds and the ditches and dripped heavily from the trees and the gutters and, in many different ways everywhere you went, flowed, spilled, splashed, purled, bubbled, seeped, trickled, squished underfoot in the soft spongy ground, and, in airborne form on all the cool misty days, turned the exhalations of birds into tiny vapor clouds. Water, water, drenching water everywhere, and with it the first fine smells of smells not smelled for at least four months: dirt, mud, rock, grass, waterlogged logs rotting in the weeds. *Perfume.*

This fleeting transition was my favorite time of year on the mountainside. As much as I yearned for spring and summer, I regretted seeing it end, and wished I could somehow hold on to the joyous feelings of relief, liberation, and anticipation that always came with it.

—◆—

That April, I vowed to fish the new season through only with flies I tied myself. This seemed to me a sure way to amplify and accelerate my progress as an angler, even if it meant I might not catch some fish I previously would have. When up against difficult trout whose preferred food at the moment was hard to detect, or enduring a bad run of days when nothing seemed to work, I was just going to have to do my best to figure things out and then try to manufacture a solution at my vise. In the long run, this would do me more good than simply having to make the best selection I could from the hundreds of professionally tied flies in my boxes, some of which had dwelt there since the Carter administration.

Not that I ever got fancy about it. My Adams flies, which always looked debauched, hung over, as if they'd been on a bender all night and needed a few hours' sleep and a shave, and my Red Quills, whose bodies I wound with hackle stems that, to make them soft and pliant, I took the time to soak in water, were as complicated as I got. Most of the flies I made that year were rudimentary and relatively quick to tie and mirrored the rawness of my tying skills.

Many of them were caddis patterns. In my six seasons on the upper East Branch, I always did well with caddis, perhaps even better, overall, than with the trusty Adams. Except for when the East Branch was low and warm in midsummer, there were good hatches of caddis in many different sizes, body colors, wing colors, and population densities, including such main attractions as the so-called black caddis in April, the grannom or apple caddis in May, the dark blue sedge in June, and the cinnamon caddis—aka the tan caddis or the spotted sedge—more or less throughout the season. Not counting that one year when I used only my own flies, I made extensive use, all season long, of a well-known local caddis pattern, the East Branch Special, aka the East Branch Caddis, that I bought from Dave Budin at Del-Sports in Margaretville. This simple, versatile, very effective fly consisted of a peacock herl body, mixed brown and grizzly hackle, and wings of very fine deer hair. It was tied for Dave by Preston Wool-heater of Lanesville, just up the road from Phoenicia.

For the bodies of my caddis flies, I used numerous colors and shades of dubbing, both natural—muskrat, hare's ear, beaver, etc.—and synthetic. The wings were usually undyed deer or elk hair, but sometimes I used mallard or goose quill segments tied on tent style. If I wanted to make sure a fly stayed on top, I wrapped hackle in front of the wings. Often, though, I didn't bother with hackle. Nor did I ever palmer these flies. I tied them in sizes 14 and 16, occasionally in 12, with considerable variation in the thickness of the bodies.

The trout reacted very well to these ultrasimple flies in grays, browns, tans, creams, and yellows. They would grab them off the top in riffles and other moving water, strike them below the surface on the swing, and even jump clear out of the water for them the second they landed. They seemed most responsive when the flies were presented not high and dry or entirely submerged but in the surface film. One late-May evening they attacked a mustard-yellow fly so voraciously that they stripped almost all the deer hair from it. On another May evening they similarly demolished a caddis I'd tied using beaver hair.

But most of all they seemed to like these flies in shades of green, ranging from dark olive to bright apple. This held true on the East Branch all season long. That fall I also caught some good rainbows on the Esopus with these same Green Caddis, fishing them over and down in fast water. To this day I always make sure there are at least a few Green Caddis in my fly boxes no matter where or when I go fishing.

I wish I could say that my use of these caddis flies and my tying of them were the result of my own observations and resourcefulness, but in fact they originated in a book I read called *Meeting & Fishing the Hatches* by the late Charles Meck. Recounting some of his experiences fishing caddis patterns on the Little Juniata River and Bowman's Creek in Pennsylvania, Meck writes:

I once met a real expert fly fisherman on the same Little Juniata River. This man took more trout and larger trout than any other fisherman on the stream. On several occasions when he was fishing I sat back and watched. He was not one to come over and converse, but he mechanically went on with his expert skill of casting, catching, and releasing trout. Finally, on about the third or fourth meeting, I asked him what pattern he used. "Caddis—nothing but caddis. Day in, day out they catch more fish for me," he said as he showed me his Green Caddis imitation.

This passage stuck with me. It highlighted the *simplicity* that was one of my earliest fly-fishing ideals. Furthermore, Meck provided easy instructions for making deer-hair caddis flies, which he said he had learned from Barry Beck, the well-known Pennsylvania angler. Even a self-taught tying tyro like me could make one of these flies in very little time, so I started tying them and catching fish with them. Thank you, Mr. Meck.

I also did well that year fishing a ridiculously simple, home-recipe wet fly during the evening sulphur hatches: some blended yellow and orange polypropylene dubbing on a size 16 or 14 hook, quill-segment wings from just about any feather that happened to be handy, and maybe a wisp or two of hackle or deer hair to heighten the bugginess. Trout hit these wet flies hard and seemed much to prefer them to my dries. That summer, another fly I put to good use was one I called the White Adams, whose only difference from my standard Adams was that its body was white poly instead of muskrat. I don't recall tying any yellow, orange, green, tan, brown, or black Adamses, but we all know that in the right place at the right time, each of them would have worked.

That fishing season, my fourth on the upper East Branch, was an outstanding one in the Catskills, as timely rains kept the freestone rivers full, cool, and fishable for more of the year than usual. It was also my best season so far. I caught more and better fish and had fewer skunkings. Even the chubs were a little bigger that year.

I attributed my better results not to my humble homemade flies—trout aren't that stupid—but to the unusually good fishing conditions. I'm sure most Catskill anglers benefited just as much as I did. Nevertheless, there were fine fleeting moments that year when I allowed myself to think that perhaps something excellent was happening, that all my hours on the East Branch were finally paying off in subtly but significantly improved skills, and that my growing familiarity with the river was actually beginning—*beginning*—to deepen into something approaching knowledge and, dare I say it, insight.

One evening that June I went exploring for a new spot to fish in the most densely wooded, most secluded part of the East Branch between Margaretville and the Pepacton, a pathless area abounding with thorns, snags, foot-catching roots, face-whipping branches, entangling vines, poison ivy, bees, and delirious mosquitoes. You really had to stay in the water just to get around. The river didn't pass through this little jungle in a single flow, but was broken up into strands and connecting channels and isolated backwater pools and pockets of supremely trouty water that looked and felt as if they had never been fished. They assuredly had been, of course. This was not the remote wilderness; New York City was only 140 miles away, and the muffled sound of invisible motor vehicles came through from the other side of the woods. Still, I had never seen another fisherman poking around in there, and it was entirely possible that some of that superb trout habitat had not been fished for many years.

I waded up-current in a swift little creek that turned out to be the drainage of a surprisingly deep pool about sixty feet long and two-thirds as wide. The banks of the pool were high and impassable, clogged with willow thickets and impenetrable undergrowth and strewn with pretty clusters of dame's rocket, both pink and white, whose perfume is said to intensify in the evening and truly seemed to be doing so that night. Two or three very old blowdowns rotted in the water. The pool felt strangely private, off-limits; it had an atmosphere, a mood, of separateness from the river of which it was a part. At first I felt weirdly like a trespasser, an intruder, a feeling reinforced by the beaver that whacked the water with its tail as I moved into casting position, waist-deep at the outflow end.

I had a batch of newly made Adams dries and tied on a size 14. There were no naturals in the air or on the water and no signs of trout I could detect. But I had to make only a few casts toward the head of the pool before the first fish came up and snatched the Adams on its downstream drift. Yes! The moment that never gets old. It was a solid upper East Branch brown trout, eleven inches long, built like a warrior, and it fought with that fierce, thrashing, defiant strength that never ceases to impress us, jumping high out of the water two or three times before I could bring it in and calm it down—I was not carrying a net—and gently release it back into the depths.

Over the next hour and a half in that pool, I caught seven more of those leaping, churning, live-free-or-die battlers, a few of them a little bigger than the first, a few a little smaller. The first seven of my eight trout took the same Adams, after which it was so chewed up I had to tie on a fresh one. The eighth trout swallowed the fly so deep I had to snip the tippet and let the fish keep it. If those trout had ever seen an artificial fly before, I'm Izaak Walton.

Of all the hundreds of times I fished the East Branch during my six years in Margaretville, that June evening was one of the experiences that I remember most vividly and that left me most gratified. It was, to me, a fundamental type of fly-fishing perfection: the successful casting of dry flies, not just any dry flies but Adams dry flies, not just Adams dries but Adams dries I had tied myself, upstream to hard-striking, hard-fighting, high-leaping brown trout in a solitary place so in keeping with my idea of trout stream beauty and mystery that I felt extravagantly blessed just to be there, fishing or not. But there was where I was, doing this thing that was inherently worth doing the way it was supposed to be done and the way I had hoped I would one day do it way back when I started. It sounds so elementary, but if you're an angler, it means so much and is so profoundly rewarding.

～━━・～

Still, as I left the pool and started the long wade upstream in the darkness, I felt a vague, familiar uneasiness. I thought of the eight trout I had just caught and released, imagined them hunkered down that moment in the safe depths of their pool, wondering in whatever dim, primeval, protoplasmic way trout do what the hell had just hit them.

I thought in particular of the one that had my Adams in its throat. Would it be all right? I told myself, not for the first time, that I had to start crimping the barbs of my hooks; better yet, switch to barbless ones. The conventional wisdom was that the trout would be fine as long as the tippet was cut quickly and without excessive handling of the fish. The trout would continue to feed normally, and in time, perhaps even quickly, the hook would rust and come out.

As a committed catch-and-release angler, I was always reminding myself that the "release" part was the single most important aspect of my fly fishing. It sickened me to see a clueless fisherman holding a suffocating trout out of the water longer than was good for it just so the fisherman could get a few photos or because he couldn't get the hook out, not to mention holding the fish down on the rocks or the bank as it struggled to get free. It was one of the few things that could make me mouth off at total strangers.

I tried, not always successfully, to do it right: getting a trout to net or to hand as fast as possible, keeping it in the water, handling it minimally, not squeezing it, not touching its gills, not prolonging a difficult hook removal, then holding it facing upstream so that water would pass through its gills until it was ready to swim away. As high-minded as this sounds, it isn't always easy to pull off, what with the uncooperative, squirming trout; the often swiftly moving water; your uncertain footing; the awkwardness of your rod under one arm; the cumbersome net; the mosquito or bee in your face; your numb fingers in cold weather; and the scary sound you just heard up in the woods in grizzly country.

Nor did I delude myself into thinking that just because I was a catch-and-release man, I was the trout's bosom bud. I knew that if trout were capable of thought, they would despise me and my catch-and-release piousness. Catch and release did not exonerate me from the violence I brought to their already hard lives for no reason other than personal pleasure. Undoubtedly, some of the fish I caught and then released so conscientiously and even affectionately (murmured sweet nothings, perhaps a grateful kiss on the head) died anyway, from the exhaustion of the fight or unintentional rough handling or both. Even trout that managed to live long lives despite being caught and released multiple times often ended up so scarred that they made me think of Chuck Wepner, the "Bayonne Bleeder," after Sonny Liston got through with him at the Jersey City Armory in 1970. The times I had caught one of these banged-up survivors in the no-kill sections of the Beaverkill, I felt a kind of shame, as if I were taking my turn in a gang beating of someone already down and done in.

All this helps explain why, even though I was a confirmed catch-and-release fisherman, I was entirely in favor of keeping a few trout from time to time for a nice meal. I never did it myself anymore—catch and release had become habit—but often thought I should start again. I felt it would help keep me honest, mindful of what was really going on here. Catch and release or no catch and release, I was a predator and the trout were my victims, the losers, in one way or another, every single time. It seemed necessary to see the act through, every now and then, to its original, natural conclusion.

CHAPTER EIGHT

First stirring of change—
Out on the farm—Big drakes—
A rare sighting

THAT NEXT WINTER, MY FIFTH IN THE CABIN, I STARTED TO KNOW in my heart that something was changing. It was just a stirring at the time, the beginning of an awareness that the life I'd been living there had almost run its course, was not enough anymore. I hadn't had any idea when that first stirring would come or, frankly, even if it would. Part of me had hoped that it wouldn't, and that I would have learned instead that I had the makeup to live out my allotted pittance of days under the sun and the stars as a poor, contented, unshaven, property-rejecting, rat-race-renouncing, cigarette-rolling, whiskey-drinking, rust-bucket-driving, potter's-field-bound trout bum. Oh yes, there was a passing whiff of disappointment. But the stirring was undeniable, and I knew it was only going to grow.

It was an odd winter, the usual pipe-bursting cold interspersed with brief spells of springlike mildness. In January there was more rain than snow. One day as I walked up the muddy dirt road with my five-gallon kerosene jug in hand, headed down to the Red Barrel to fill it up, I ran into Bill. He was not his usual smiling, cheerful self; he seemed shaken, dazed. He said he'd been arrested for driving while intoxicated and had just spent two nights in the county jail up in Delhi.

Bill said he'd been drinking at Frankie's, a roadhouse in Arkville where we both liked to go, and had left it "bombed." He got into his Ford Ranger and drove it into a ditch alongside Route 28. He couldn't get it out, so he left it there and got a ride home with someone whose identity he did not remember. Then, in the middle of the night, the state police came to his cabin, got him out of bed, tested him for blood alcohol, and drove him to the jail. Bill said it was such a wretched experience that he was unable to eat anything the whole time he was there. "All the other prisoners were a bunch of young toughs," he said. "They called me Dad."

That spring, which was cool and gray, I got irregular but frequent work as a laborer on a horse farm in the New Kingston Valley, an area of surpassing pastoral beauty just north of town. By summer the work became fairly steady. At eight dollars an hour, it put more cash in my pocket than I'd had since moving to Margaretville. I'd given up my cooking job but had found another modest but reliable source of income as a freelance contributor to the *Woodstock Times*, the weekly newspaper in that famous small town not far away in Ulster County. Just as important as the extra money this gave me was the writing outlet and the connection once again with like-minded people who spoke the beautiful old language of print newspapers, as lovely a language to me as the language of fly fishing. Now, daily experience was not just that but—blessed word—*material*, too.

I'd work on the farm from eight in the morning until five or six and then go straight to the river and fish till dark, sometimes well after dark. Eventually, though, another summer drought set in and the East Branch became warm, low, and slow and never came all the way back that season. A local guy with whom I often worked on the farm, Jeb, had lived in the Margaretville area all his life and told me that some of the days that summer were the hottest he had ever experienced.

The farm was situated along a rough, unpaved road, well off the nearest blacktop, about eleven miles from my cabin. Only four horses (dressage) were resident there at the time, but the work necessary to keep them healthy and happy and to maintain the property never stopped. I spent endless hours on what farmers call picking rock: clearing pasture, by hand, of the many thousands of stones that just keep coming to the surface year after year and that long ago gave rise to the regional description of the soil as "two stones for every dirt." I'd load up my wheelbarrow with stones, many of them small boulders, then push the wheelbarrow across the field and dump the stones into the big shovel of a backhoe for transport to stone-pile central. Then repeat, and repeat, and repeat. I cleared brush, dug postholes, stacked hay bales in the barn, brought hay to the horses in the pasture, sometimes mucked their stalls, worked on the construction of a riding arena, mowed grass, weed-whacked weeds, and did all manner of other jobs.

The aforementioned Jeb, though not a big man, had the strength and endurance for long hard days in the sun of an ox, and no matter how close my arms felt to falling off or my legs to buckling, no matter how parched my throat, it was a point of honor with me to try to keep up with him, though I didn't have the advantage of the Christian songs he sometimes softly sang while digging postholes and picking rock.

When I started working at the farm, I was largely indifferent to horses, seeing them as inscrutable and perhaps stupid. But I grew to be very fond of the four horses whose stalls I cleaned and whose hay and water and little treats I brought them, and to believe that, like dogs, cats, and parakeets I had known, they possessed a sentience, a character, and a sense of humor that compared favorably to those of some of the people I'd encountered on my zigzag journey through life.

The foreman I worked under on the farm, Buck, was widely regarded locally as fearsome and intimidating, one scary dude, an image I believe he relished and cultivated. Buck was in his early forties and had the beefy, hulking, powerful build of a retired heavyweight, along with the incipient paunch and thinning hair of early middle age. Highly intelligent, phenomenally strong, a heavy smoker, bearing maybe a half-dozen tattoos, Buck had a withering glower and plenty of stories about the men he had crushed with his fists, including the one he hit so hard at the start of a fight that the guy was out cold for twenty minutes and Buck thought he was dead.

"Most people around here are terrified of me," Buck told me. "I am not a man to be trifled with."

"Everybody around here is afraid of Buck," the owner of the farm told me.

Buck had a vivid, colorful way of talking in which I heard echoes of the distant agricultural past of rural New York State:

"I use my left eye as a level and my right eye as a plumb bob."

"Best thing since pockets on a shirt."

"This drill don't have enough ass in its britches."

"It was colder'n a well digger's ass."

"It's gonna rain like a cow pissin' on a flat rock."

"I cut that thing finer'n frog hair."

He once referred to the farm as "the asshole of nowhere," but the setting was gorgeous and I loved being there and getting sunburned and smelling the fields, the hay, and the horse shit all day and building relationships with the horses and the many happy dogs that had the run of the place. My hands grew calluses so thick and hard that, no matter the task, work gloves were not needed. There was a pump on the farm that drew the coldest, purest, best-tasting water imaginable up from the ground, and after shoveling, digging, raking, chopping, hauling, swinging a pickax or a sledgehammer, wielding a crowbar, and pushing heavy wheelbarrows all day in the blistering sun, that water running down my throat and over my face and head and down the back of my neck was better than any ice-cold beer I ever had.

One night that year in late June, just as it had become too dark to comfortably keep fishing, I was walking upstream along the bank, back to my car, when I saw something I hadn't seen in my previous four seasons on the East Branch. It was happening out in the middle of the river, where some sort of bashed-up, unidentifiable metal object that had washed downstream years ago had long been securely lodged. The object—I think it might have been a commercial sign—was almost entirely underwater, and had the effect of slowing the current almost to a halt and creating a sizable pocket of barely moving water on the downstream side. This was one of my automatic stops on most outings. A dry fly often paid off here, and I'd also taken many good fish drifting nymphs and wet flies through the seams on each side of the slack.

But this was the first time I had seen what I was seeing now in the remaining light of the sky. In the area of still water created by the obstruction, trout were feasting on large, light-colored mayflies, as big as or bigger than any flies I'd ever seen on the East Branch. This activity did not seem to be occurring anywhere else. Given the dim light and my distance from the flies and the fish, I couldn't really tell if it was a hatch or a spinner fall or both. But I had no trouble seeing that the flies were unusually big and the trout, turned on.

I felt both the excitement of discovery and considerable perplexity. How could I not have seen this until my fifth season on the East Branch? How could that be? Add to the excitement and perplexity a dollop of chagrin.

When I got home, I searched through my fishing notes. The previous year, in late June, I had written: "A few very big flies were leaving the water tonight. Mothlike in color." Two years before that, on two occasions in July, I had noted "a few *huge* duns" (I'd underlined the adjective) and "big whitish mayflies," both times at or just before dark. On none of those nights, though, did I see anything like the moderately heavy concentration of mayflies I had just seen, with trout scarfing them down. I suppose it was the extreme sparseness of the past appearances, combined with the darkness, that kept me from paying more attention to the flies.

At any rate, this time I made a point in the following days, before the drought really set in, of being on the river just before and after dark with my eyes peeled. The big flies were always around, though not as conspicuously as on the first night, and I did have some good dry-fly fishing. In color the flies were not so much "mothlike" or "whitish" as, it seemed to me, shades of yellow. The trout weren't terribly fussy about artificials: they would take yellow or cream flies in size 12—the biggest dry flies I had—even though the naturals were at least a size bigger. One or two trout even took a bushy-looking Adams variant on the same-size hook.

Based on my reference books, I knew these flies had to be either yellow drakes or golden drakes, two of the common names for, respectively, *Ephemera varia* and *Anthopotamus distinctus* (the latter being known at the time, and until fairly recently, as *Potamanthus distinctus*). It's also possible I was seeing both flies, since they have much in common besides their size and fetching appearance. They hatch basically at the same time of year and the same time of day, and they're both at home in slower, warmer water. Somehow I managed not to learn at the time, as I subsequently did, that the golden drake is easy to distinguish from the yellow by the middle of its three tails, which is noticeably shorter than the other two. Also, experts say the body of the yellow drake is actually more off-white or cream than yellow.

As for my tardiness in becoming fully aware of these flies on the East Branch, maybe I can draw at least a little comfort from Paul Weamer's comments on yellow and golden drakes in his book *Fly-Fishing Guide to the Upper Delaware River*. Weamer notes that hatches of the yellow drake "are usually sparse," while those of the golden drake can be "unreliable" and "differ from year to year"; indeed, "some years, the bugs barely show themselves, and the trout seem to ignore the few flies that do hatch."

Still, my experience with these flies stayed with me as an example of how it is impossible to be too attentive, too curious, on a trout river. There is so much out there to see—as long as we have the eyes to see it. So much to see and so much to miss seeing. I am always aware when fly fishing that not just my angling skills but also my faculties for observation and perception are being tested. It is so much more than just a sport, a recreation. If that's all it were, I'd probably collect butterflies or buy a telescope and gaze at the stars instead. I need a deep mental involvement in the things I do. I would say first and foremost to any novice fly fisher: Don't become preoccupied with your gear or how far you can cast or how many fish you catch. Learn to see, and know what it is you're seeing, and remember it.

—◦—

By the last week of September, the river had cooled but was still remarkably low. I went out there one evening after a day of heavy rain that hardly seemed to raise the water an inch. The season on the East Branch was about to end, and I just wanted to throw a line. All I did was cast a Green Caddis over and down and let it drift into the swing—fly fishing a child could do after a few minutes' instruction. I actually caught a couple of small, dopey trout.

As I was standing still on the fringe of the water watching the progress of my fly, a large animal emerged from the brush maybe two hundred feet downstream on the other side of the river. I froze and watched. I was thrilled: There was only one animal that big in the Catskill Mountains. I was finally seeing a bear in the wild, a sight that had escaped me, almost unbelievably, in all my years of tramping through the Catskill woods and wading the Catskill rivers and living on the margin of the state forest, an area where stories of bears raiding chicken coops and bird feeders, not to mention the occasional kitchen, were routine. I was a little surprised that this particular black bear did not appear to be black; it looked to me to be light brown or tan. Then again, I'd read that some black bears actually have brown, blond, or cinnamon coats, so light brown or tan did not seem a stretch.

After poking around briefly at the edge of the brush, the animal started walking slowly over the drought-year expanse of exposed river-bottom stones toward the stream, allowing me to see it entirely and clearly in profile. Now I was confused. Bears didn't have long, flowing tails like that. And that wasn't a bear's body. Nor was that a bear's head. The long, bushy tail; the supple, streamlined body; the graceful, slightly mincing way the animal moved; the head—all these things were unmistakably feline.

It was a cat, a very, very big cat. I had just become one of a small but growing number of people who had either seen or claimed to have seen a mountain lion—aka cougar, wildcat, panther, catamount, puma—in a state where the animal was long ago officially declared "extirpated." Calling the New York State Department of Environmental Conservation to report a cougar sighting wasn't quite as bad for one's credibility as calling the police to report a flying saucer, but it was close.

The cougar reached the stream, which was hardly more than ankle-deep at that point and only fifteen or twenty feet wide, and crossed it, appearing to me to take its time and to look for the best places to step. Then it effortlessly leaped up into the undergrowth of the rather high bank and was gone. If it kept going in that direction, it would soon have emerged from the woods along Route 28.

The sighting had lasted about ninety seconds. I'd had a sustained, focused, unobstructed look at that animal. Knowing that I was not supposed to be seeing what I was in fact seeing, and that the Department of Environmental Conservation would politely push back when I reported it, I had looked hard and carefully and had even told myself to be sure I wasn't hallucinating. As soon as I got home, I wrote down everything I'd seen so I wouldn't forget it.

It *was* a mountain lion. The state's official position was that no one had produced incontestable evidence—roadkill, scat, paw prints, hair, the remains of a deer killed in the way characteristic of mountain lions—that the animals existed in the Catskills or the Adirondacks or anywhere else in New York State. Conservation officials maintained that reported "sightings" were usually just the fevered misidentifications of domestic cats and dogs, bobcats, and mangy coyotes. They did, however, leave open the possibility that people might have seen cougars that had been living in captivity, either legally or illegally, and then either escaped or, once their owners saw what that cute little cub they'd bought was growing into, were released into the wild. But there was no self-sustaining population of cougars in New York State, of that the wildlife authorities were adamant.

So it's entirely possible—OK, probable—that the mountain lion I saw had spent most of its life in a cage, perhaps as some bozo's "pet."

But knowing that did not weaken the jolt of what I saw that evening while fishing the East Branch no more than a mile from the center of Margaretville. I saw something that was not supposed to be seeable: the ancient sight of a mountain lion on the prowl in the Catskill forest. It was as close as I ever expect to come to seeing a ghost.

In subsequent years there were credible stories of other cougar sightings in the same Pepacton–East Branch area, which made me smile when I learned about them. I know what I saw. So if you are ever fishing some secluded part of the upper East Branch between Margaretville and the Pepacton and it gets late and dark and you've got a long walk through the forest and the brush back to your car—well, good luck!

CHAPTER NINE

Stalled out—The Flood of '96—
Moving into town—A river made over—
Fishing in town—The state of my gear—
Leaving

December number six in my cabin on Pakatakan Mountain. Once again the light-starved days, no sooner born than starting to wilt and die; the clear plastic duct-taped over the windows, the heavy quilt hanging between the temperate living room and the arctic kitchen; the bigger bills and the fewer ways to make the money to pay them; the end of all fishing, of river solace, for at least four months, probably longer. December always brought a feeling of shrinkage and withdrawal, of retreat into my mountainside redoubt for the long slog to April, fortified by adequate supplies of firewood, kerosene, copper water pipe, and cheap alcohol in several different forms.

But that December brought something else: a return, much stronger this time, more insistent, of the sense I'd had the previous winter that all this was just about over, that the time to move on was getting close. It became even more pronounced as December slid into January. By the middle of that month, I had a premature but whopping case of cabin fever—or was it something deeper?

My circumstances felt oppressively, stupidly redundant, stalled out, utterly lacking in that sense of progress toward something better or more important that we want our lives to have, even if it's only an illusion. Materially I was just as bad off as I'd been the day I moved into the cabin five and a half years earlier, even worse because of growing credit-card debt. I knew I wouldn't be able to stand it if yet another December came around and, even if in the name of the abounding beauties of fly fishing for trout, I was still warming myself by the kerosene heater and glancing at the stack of unpayable bills on the desk and scrounging all over Delaware and Ulster and Greene Counties for six-dollar-an-hour work. Clearly I had just about reached the limits of my desire to live the marginal life of a hand-to-mouth Catskill Mountains fly fisherman.

I didn't even have a car anymore. My Mazda, completing an abrupt and financially irreversible decline that began with a collapsed strut and ended with a failed fuel pump, had coasted silently to its final rest that October on Route 28 in Boiceville, where I surrendered it to the owner of a service station. I had tried to replace it with the aging blue Oldsmobile now parked in the driveway, bought for two hundred dollars—all I could scrape up—from the husband of a checkout woman at the A&P. But you get what you pay for, and the Blue Bomber, though it was kind of cool-looking and had a spotless, perfumy interior, had already shown that I'd paid about twice what it was worth. I didn't dare drive it anymore. Eventually I just gave it to a guy I knew who wanted a project car.

I needed wheels. I needed to be able to go to a doctor and a dentist. I longed for enough heat for a change that I'd be able to lounge around half naked all winter. I wanted to take fishing trips to Wyoming and Montana. I needed to be there financially for my aging parents. I needed a more complex, more complicated life again. I wanted to compete again. Hell, I wanted something I hadn't had in sixteen years: a real job, full-time, with bennies.

Also, I'd had more than enough of the person I was confined in that cabin with for yet another long winter: my own long-haired, rarely shaven, kerosene-scented self. The self: that best of best friends; that perfect secret-keeper and confidant; that most trusted adviser;

that most intimate, loving, loyal, and accommodating of companions; that prison, that junkyard, that clogged drain, that babbling bore, that flat tire on the interstate, that rat in the wall in the middle of the night. I'd had a big enough dose, thanks. There wasn't room in that cabin anymore for the two of us.

Still, even with all of the above, giving up the East Branch and my angling-centered life was going to be hard. It was also going to require some planning and preparation. So I decided to give myself one more trout season, one more April-through-September, and then to be gone before the start of another winter. Just making this decision made me feel better.

That December and January it seemed to snow without stop. By mid-January the walls of shoveled snow lining the narrow path I kept having to clear up through the yard must already have been five feet high. So much snow had piled up that people worried their roofs would collapse, and I made sure word got around that for a reasonable charge I would mount any roof with a shovel and remove the snow, taking care not to go over the edge with it. Since I no longer had a car, this meant miles of walking. Add to all the walking and shoveling the occasional round-trip bicycle trek of more than twenty miles out to the horse farm for a day's work, if the roads were clear, and at least I was getting my exercise. If you want to get fit, move to the sticks and sell your car.

Then came a day, January 19, of freakishly warm air and hard, steady rain. All that snow was melting fast. I donned my clear plastic rain suit and stepped out into the murk.

As I followed the path up the sloping yard toward the driveway, my car, the barely functional Blue Bomber with the overly air-freshened interior, looked odd; something was different. Then I saw that its wheels were buried almost to the bumpers in mud and silt being carried by a turbulent little river that sped left to right down the gradient where the dirt road had been, a result of the tremendous amount of snowmelt pouring down off Pakatakan Mountain in combination with the driving rain. What had been my dirt road was now a gouged-out channel, as much as two feet deep, through which ran this fast, dirty, hideous little river.

I made my way along the edge of the torrent up to where the dirt road was still intact, in front of Bill's place. Bill was outside, marveling at the speed and profuseness of the melting. Curious about what might be happening down below along Route 28 and the East Branch, we got into his pickup and started down the hill. This was a mistake. Water was rushing down the mountain on both sides of the road and taking chunks of the blacktop with it. We turned around and went back up the hill while we still had a road and Bill still had a truck.

The next morning was sunny, beautiful, innocent. I went down through the woods to Route 28 and walked to town—or what was left of it. The East Branch had receded into its channel, if only barely, but was still racing and surging and lapping at the banks, still so scary you didn't want to get anywhere near it. It was a filthy, ugly, trash-filled, malignant-looking brown, wholly unrecognizable as my lucent, murmuring stream of soft June evenings when the brown trout flashed, the mists rose, and the whitetails stole down to the water's edge to sip.

The commercial area next to Route 28 was in ruins. The East Branch had gutted the A&P, the drugstore, and the Soap 'n' Suds laundromat. The Bun 'n' Cone restaurant was a sagging, buckling heap. A front wall had been blown out of the carpet and tile store. The East Branch had completely chewed up the big main parking lot, leaving a field of rubble. It had demolished the Citgo station and carried away the pumps. It had picked up a Dumpster and smashed it into a tree. A little downstream, a car lay upside down in the river. The trees and bushes on the riverbanks had netted a fantastic amount of rubbish: bottles, cans, sneakers, jackets, toys, coolers, tarps, towels, tires, brooms, rugs, plywood, pillows, umbrellas, signs, magazines, plastic buckets, plastic trash bags, plastic this, plastic that—lots of plastic.

On Main Street, a little farther away from the river and a little higher up, the destruction was almost as great, as the rising East Branch floodwater had combined with spillover from a couple of smaller in-town streams to inundate that part of the business district. In the days after the flood, Main Street was an eerily quiet place lined with growing piles of rubble and ruined belongings from people's businesses and homes.

I spent a lot of time in the village during those days, gathering information to use in articles for the *Woodstock Times*. Although I was unhurt in any way by the flood, the losses inflicted on so many people, the sights and smells of the devastated village, the befouled river, and the slummy riverbanks, only fed the gloom I'd been warring with that winter. On a much lesser scale of personal loss, maybe the East Branch had carried away something of my life, too.

Since money was as low as ever and my prospect of getting a vehicle just about nil, I decided to move into town for my last season on the East Branch, an easy enough proposition for someone with as few possessions as I had. The fishing came first, and for an angler limited to his feet and a bicycle for getting around, living in the village—the river ran right through it—made the most sense. It would have been impossible to get in my usual time astream living carless way up on that mountainside. I looked forward to the change anyway.

True, I wasn't going to have as much of the beauty and the solitude I'd grown so accustomed to fishing in, but I was a beggar now, not a chooser, and for fishing purposes it was the exact same river—same trout, same flies, same clean water, same fine laboratory for fly-fishing learning and advancement. Nor would I have to give up my favorite stretches of the river altogether—it wasn't that long a bicycle ride to reach them.

So I got a short-term lease on a spacious apartment in the middle of town and moved in that May. Compared with the cabin, the apartment, though it cost no more, was luxurious: soft wall-to-wall carpeting, stairs leading up to a loft bedroom, big windows, a modern kitchen. Where was my smoking jacket? At first I enjoyed the novelty of such comfort, but I knew I was just killing time and hardly bothered to unpack, living all the while I was there out of cardboard boxes and duffel bags.

The apartment's one drawback was that it was noisy, situated as it was right over the sidewalk (second floor) and the busy village traffic, with a panoramic view of the recovering riverside shopping area— the real hub of Margaretville. I liked the early-morning quacking of ducks that came from the Binnekill, the small stream adjacent to Main Street, and the pleasing *ting . . . ting . . . ting* of horseshoes being thrown in the pit over at the Bull Run Tavern. But after almost six years of silence in the cabin, I had trouble adjusting to the hubbub of cars, trucks, and voices. I can't pretend I wasn't interested at times in the relationship drama being acted out on the other side of the living room wall, but I hated having to hear it. I much preferred the sounds of red squirrels on the cabin roof and of animals snarling and fighting underneath the floor, fights that sometimes ended with the smell of skunk rising up through the floor like a gathering cloud and filling the whole house. Not bad at all once you get used to it.

Being able to walk to and from the bars in just minutes was convenient and fun but ultimately of dubious value. I had more hangovers now, even less money in my pocket, and, a couple of times, spirited new acquaintances hailing me from the street at grievous hours. I had traveled maybe a mile as the crow flies, but it was a different life.

On my first trips that spring to my familiar East Branch haunts between Margaretville and the reservoir, I found a river much changed by the January floodwater. Rivers always vary at least a little from one season to the next, but this was a real makeover.

Several of my favorite pools and deadfalls were gone, though good-looking new ones had appeared elsewhere. Huge deposits of stones and gravel borne downstream by the prodigious currents had created new shoals and banks and changed the character of the flow. Banks had been recut. Pools had become runs; runs had become pools. Two old beaver homes where I'd often fished had been carried off. Even those features of the river that remained essentially the same had been altered in some way. If anything, it seemed to me, the amount of good trout habitat had increased.

But the fishing would be terrible that season, even though water levels and temperatures were good for almost the whole summer. Hatches were sparse or seemed to be missing altogether, as the churning currents during the flood dislodged the river-bottom stones and ground to death, or at least swept away, countless mayflies and caddis flies in their immature, preemergent forms, not to mention trout eggs from the previous fall's spawning season.

Few good trout seemed to have hung around. Often there didn't appear to be anything left in the river but the small hatchery trout from the spring stocking. One view I heard expressed a few times was that the good fish had dropped down to the reservoir during the flood and stayed there. "I haven't caught shit all season," several local fishermen told me, using basically the same words.

In addition, bank reconstruction, dredging of silt and stone left behind by the floodwater, and other post-flood work being done at various places along the river further disrupted the streambed life and discolored the water downstream, making the bad fishing even worse.

Nevertheless, I was determined to make the most of my final season on the East Branch, and spent as much time on the river that year as I had all the others. The rare occasions when I met a reasonably good hatch or spinner fall were like beholding a small miracle. One night in early June, for example, I encountered a heavy swarm of spinners, many of which bore conspicuous egg sacs. I didn't much doubt that these were the so-called big sulphurs, *Ephemerella invaria*. But how did such supremely delicate creatures survive the ruinous convulsions of January? I was impressed. At any rate, there didn't seem to be a single trout around to take advantage of them.

Because of my yellow drake/golden drake experience of the previous summer, I watched for them this year and was delighted to see a few over the river just before dark one night in late June. So they, too, had shown some resilience.

❧

At first I regularly bicycled between the village and my usual stretches of the East Branch, which I really did not want to give up. But the round trips of up to two miles or so were time-consuming and, with rod, vest, and chest waders in tow, increasingly a bother. The return trip was usually in the dark. So it wasn't long before I opted almost always for the convenience of fishing in town, especially in that part of the river that was literally a five-minute walk from my apartment.

In the previous five-plus seasons, I had fished the water in town only a handful of times. It had never much interested me as trout water. More important, I hadn't moved to the mountains, put fly fishing at the center of my life, washed dishes, boiled linguine, chopped vegetables, split wood, picked rock, dug postholes, raked horse shit, and shoveled snow off roofs for the privilege of fishing with the Route 28 traffic on one side of me and the bustle of village life on the other, though admittedly neither was exactly megalopolitan in intensity.

But that was then. Now I became a regular fisherman on that length of the East Branch running, roughly speaking, from the little park behind Main Street upstream under the Bridge Street Bridge and past the town field to an area just downstream of Brookside Hardware.

And it wasn't bad at all. In fact, I was a little surprised by how easy it was to be fishing now not in the privacy of the woods but, basically, right inside the community's public space. But I shouldn't have been. By that point in my angling life, I should have known that any trout water, no matter the setting, had an unfailing power to preoccupy me, to drive everything else competing for attention inside my clamorous skull to the margins of consciousness. Whenever I stepped into a river and waded out into it, it was like passing through an invisible membrane into an adjacent world where the hypnotic time-as-water flow of the river, the brain-cleansing sound of it, the benign monomania of the search for trout, the absorption in the life cycles of bugs, the challenges of casting and presentation, all the engrossing intricacies of trying to fit undetected into the natural world, which is what the angler must do to succeed—all these things seized my mind and wouldn't let it go, even when an eighteen-wheeler hauling plywood to Oneonta went roaring by. Half the time I didn't even hear it.

Not that it wasn't different fishing in town, for it certainly was. One evening I had the jarring experience of fishing next to the town field when some sort of loud, exuberant Christian gathering began, filling the air over the river with amplified call-and-response: "Gimme a J!" "J!" "Gimme an E!" "E!" "Gimme an S! . . ." There was Christian rock music and people swaying back and forth, arms aloft. I got skunked that night and was forced to leave the river just before dark by hundreds of fluttering bats.

Another evening I looked up from the river and saw, on the other side of the invisible membrane, two attractive women sitting on the bank watching me. An audience! I knew neither but recognized both—eventually you recognize just about everyone in a village of 639 people. One of them gave me a friendly little wave. My exalted invisible membrane collapsed pathetically into the river and drifted away like Saran Wrap, just another lame, pretentious, pseudoliterary fly-fishing conceit. I appealed to the resident East Branch spirits for a fish at this time. *Any fish*, I silently pleaded, *any fish at all, even a pumpkinseed, even a chub, a seven-inch chub, I'll make it look bigger and stronger, I'll make this old rod bend, I'll give those gals a show, I'll look like Lee Wulff landing an Atlantic salmon from where they're sitting. . . .*

But the river spirits denied me, no doubt because I had recently been experimenting with a strike indicator while nymphing. These were Catskill river spirits, after all—purists. And before long my audience, probably bored, left.

One memorable fishing experience I had on the village water took place just upstream of the town field, next to a pasture where some cows were grazing, on a brilliant August afternoon.

The water, at a good level and temperature for August, had at first seemed empty of trout, as rivers often do on bright summer days. Not a fly was in the air. After slowly working my way downstream with a nymph and rousing nothing, I decided I might as well get in some dry-fly casting practice. So I tied on a size 16 dry and began casting it upstream, figuring I'd work my way back up to where I had started and then call it a day.

The only reason I chose the fly I did was that it was one of a small batch I had recently tied and I wanted to see if it rode the water properly. It was an improvised fly, matching no pattern I was aware of. Its body was brown hackle quill, stripped, its wings dyed mallard substitute for lemon wood duck. It had reddish-brown hackle at the wings and for the tail. Knitting everything together, and culminating in a most conspicuous little head behind the hook eye, was bright red thread. Both the reddish hackle and the red head stood out vividly on the water as the fly floated and bobbed ever so gently in the sun. The overall effect was intense redness.

About fifteen minutes into my casting, a fish struck the fly hard and was hooked. It was a small brown trout, eight or nine inches. I released it and cast again to the same area, and moments after the fly touched down another trout, a little bigger than the first, took it just as hard. I cast again, and the same thing happened. Over a period that could not have exceeded half an hour, in a patch of water about the size of a parking space, I caught nine thrashing, wriggling, almost uncontrollable trout, the three or four biggest about eleven inches—all on the same fly. They mangled it.

Any experienced trout fisher would have made a point of casting to that spot: The branches of a tall tree reached out over it, providing shade and falling bugs, and a strong current of bubbly water tumbled into it from a riffle. And he or she would not have been surprised to raise a fish there, especially a hatchery fish, which those trout no doubt were. But nine of them? In less than thirty minutes? I wondered if the fish were congregating around a cold spring.

As for their rather deranged assault on my fly, I have no idea what insect they thought it was. Nothing in particular, perhaps; see bug, will eat. All I do know is that my concocted, nameless, intensely red fly sparked the best half hour of fishing I had that whole meager season on the post-flood East Branch.

By now my gear was starting to show the effects of six seasons of constant fishing and tramping through the woods and brush. Apart from my inexpensive Red Ball boot-foot waders, which I'd had no choice but to replace at one point—you can fix leaks only so many times before you just can't fix them anymore—and my Cortland five-weight, double-taper line, which I'm sure I must have swapped out at least once, everything else was what I had arrived with in 1990.

My thirteen-year-old Fisher glass rod, a lovely deliverer of dry flies up to thirty-five, forty feet, had the usual dings and battle scars that rods pick up over the years, but on the whole its brown finish had stood up impressively well. I had used this rod hard, many hundreds of times, subjecting it to all manner of falls, dunkings, bangings on rocks, wanderings through dense woods, ensnarings in trees and briar bushes, yankings of snagged lines, and squeezings fully assembled into small cars. But it had withstood it all and was still perfectly sound, casting as well as ever. The spigot ferrule, line guides, caramel-colored wrappings, and deeply stained cigar-style grip were as good as they'd been the day I bought the rod.

Granted, there were issues with the copper-colored reel seat. The end cap had fallen off one evening into a couple of feet of East Branch water and disappeared. I'd replaced it with—what else?—duct tape. The downlocking ring often got stuck now when I tried to turn it, requiring me to use pliers and WD-40. But during fishing season I rarely took my rod down or removed the reel from it anyway. The idea was—or had been, before my Mazda croaked—to have the rod always in the car, strung up and ready, for the inevitable day when I would drive by a stream and see trout feeding on a great hatch and have to pull over and leap into action. Predictably, I suppose, that day never came.

My Orvis Battenkill Mark III reel was the same age as the Fisher rod but looked much older, more like a reel you might see in a display of some venerated, long-dead angler's gear at the Catskill Fly Fishing Center & Museum in Livingston Manor, a few miles from Roscoe. If I do say so, it had character. I had never babied it among the streamside rocks and midstream boulders. One of the tips of its foot had broken off, but I could still attach it securely to the rod and it still worked flawlessly.

My tan vest was in its fourteenth or fifteenth year and looked it. A couple of times I'd found years-old snack food lodged deep in a corner of the big back pocket, moldering. Had it ever been laundered? I cannot honestly say. Maybe once, but I doubt it.

In those years I just didn't give much thought to my fishing gear, as long as it worked. Nor did I think much about all the superior tackle I saw for sale in the fly shops. Even the very finest, most beautiful, most expensive rods and reels, the ones most widely coveted by fly fishermen, meant little more to me than they did to someone who didn't even fish. They were way too far beyond my financial reality to be of more than passing interest. I no more entertained thoughts of owning an elegant cane rod, or a Winston IM6 graphite, or a Hardy Perfect reel, than I did of owning a Rolls-Royce or a house in Beverly Hills. I just didn't think about these things. I had learned not only to make do with what I had but to like it, and I did.

I told myself that the most important part of an angler's tackle anyway was that ordinary little fly at the end of the tippet: selecting it, presenting it, controlling it. That was what induced a trout to strike, wasn't it? Not the fisherman's high-tech rod, big-ticket reel, superslick line, state-of-the-art vest, guide-quality breathable waders, English fly box, heirloom-quality maple net, stylish long-bill cap with neck cape, or titanium watch water-resistant to two hundred feet. As pleasing and useful as those things were, they had no clout with the trout. In the end, the delicate interplay of fly and water was all. Fly and water, water and fly. If I didn't get that part of it right, all the other stuff, even if I had it, would be a little embarrassing.

———

I fished right up to closing day, September 30. Five days later, having put my belongings in storage, I left town.

In my final months in Margaretville, I never once doubted that I had to leave. Only a MacArthur Fellowship for fly fishing could have changed my mind, but I'd begun to lose all hope for that.

It soon became clear, though, that I had left a big piece of myself behind. Often in the following months my sleep was filled with images of running water and snow. The running water included a majestic waterfall on the mountainside across the dirt road from my cabin, which of course did not exist in real life. One night I dreamed I was rolling around in deep snow in the front yard of the cabin, but the snow was warm and dry and luxurious. I heard Bill's wind chimes in my sleep. I saw the mountain lion, the fields of pink and white dame's rocket on the banks of the East Branch, a muskrat swimming with a little bouquet of dame's rocket in its mouth, the fog over the river on sunny subzero mornings.

Apart from lots of words on paper, I had absolutely nothing tangible to show for those six years, but I did have that river and that place in me and I had them for good. Much later, long after I'd restored myself materially and was living a thoroughly comfortable life, there were times when I had to admit to myself that I was not commensurately happier than I'd been while living in the cabin on Pakatakan Mountain, flat broke but so immersed in the angling life that being broke was just a minor inconvenience. Not that I ever wanted to live that way again. No, ma'am.

Spending six years on the East Branch had not burned off any of my enthusiasm for my chosen sport. It had only reinforced what I'd already long known: that it would be very hard for me to live without it, that the ability and the liberty to pursue it would be a requirement in all of life's important decisions—jobs, places of living, even relationships. Angling was and always would be as much necessity as pleasure, one of the primary ways I experienced my brief, astounding, incomprehensible turn in consciousness and light.

I still have moments, just as I did back in those East Branch days, when I'm alone on a trout stream on a beautiful afternoon or evening and hear myself thinking, almost to the point of saying it out loud: *This is it. This is as good as it gets. This is as good as it's ever going to get, any of it.* And even now I'm susceptible to that old escapist reverie, dating back forty seasons or so to my first, most impassioned years as a fly fisherman, of vanishing into the life of a full-time nomadic trout bum, of just surrendering to it unconditionally and accepting all the consequences.

It's pure fantasy, of course; I don't really want to do it and never did. But all it takes is a glimpse of a pretty stream reaching seductively into the green distance when I pass over a highway bridge, or the panoramic view from an airplane of a wild river's coiled windings through an uninhabited landscape, and my imagination is kindled, my yearnings awakened. I feel the pull. I keep expecting this to weaken with time, to start to fade; but it never does.

BIBLIOGRAPHY

SOME OF THE BOOKS AND OTHER WRITINGS LISTED HERE ARE MENtioned in the text of *East Branch*. Others, while not so mentioned, I wish to acknowledge for having helped me with reliable background information in ways not always apparent in the book.

Bergman, Ray. *Trout*, 3rd ed. New York: Knopf, 1981.

Blakeslee, Mermer. *When You Live by a River*. N.p.: Narrative Library, 2012.

Burroughs, John. *Catskills and Hudson Valley Essays*. Wickford, RI: New Street Communications, 2013.

Bussy, Ethel H. "History and Stories of Margaretville and Surrounding Area." Transcribed by Gary Wyckoff Myers, 1997. Delaware County NY Genealogy and History Site. www.dcnyhistory.org/books/marghst1.html.

Caucci, Al, and Bob Nastasi. *Hatches II: A Complete Guide to the Hatches of North American Trout Streams*, collector's ed. Norwalk, CT: Easton Press, 1996.

Darbee, Harry, with Mac Francis. *Catskill Flytier*. Philadelphia: Lippincott, 1977.

Delaware County Historical Association. *Two Stones for Every Dirt: The Story of Delaware County, New York*. Fleischmanns, NY: Purple Mountain Press, 1987.

Duerden, Tim. *A History of Delaware County, New York: A Catskill Land and Its People, 1797-2007*. Fleischmanns, NY: Purple Mountain Press, 2007.

Flick, Art. *Art Flick's New Streamside Guide to Naturals and Their Imitations*. New York: Nick Lyons Books, 1983.

Francis, Austin M. *Catskill Rivers: Birthplace of American Fly Fishing*. New York: Nick Lyons Books, 1983.

Galusha, Diane. *Liquid Assets: A History of New York's Water System*, expanded ed. Fleischmanns, NY: Purple Mountain Press, 2016.

Gordon, Theodore. *The Complete Fly Fisherman: The Notes and Letters of Theodore Gordon*, edited by John McDonald. New York: Nick Lyons Books, Lyons & Burford, 1989.

Hackle, Sparse Grey [Alfred W. Miller]. *Fishless Days, Angling Nights*. Guilford, CT: Lyons Press, 2001.

Ketcham, Christopher. "Cat Eyes: The Eastern Cougar Has Been Declared Extinct. So Why Do Sightings of the Animal Persist?" *Earth Island Journal* 26, no. 2 (2011). www.earthisland.org/journal/index.php/eij/article/cat_eyes/

Lee, Art. *Fishing Dry Flies for Trout on Rivers and Streams*. New York: Atheneum, 1983.

Leiser, Eric. *The Dettes: A Catskill Legend*. Fishkill, NY: Willowkill Press, 1992.

McClane, A.J. *The Compleat McClane: A Treasury of A.J. McClane's Classic Angling Adventures*. New York: Dutton, Truman Talley Books, 1988.

McClane, A.J. *Fishing with McClane*, edited by George Reiger. Englewood Cliffs, NJ: Prentice-Hall, 1975.

McClane, A.J. *McClane's Angling World*. New York: Dutton, Truman Talley Books, 1986.

Meck, Charles R. *Meeting and Fishing the Hatches*. New York: Winchester Press, 1977.

Pobst, Dick. *Trout Stream Insects: An Orvis Streamside Guide*. New York: Lyons & Burford, 1990.

Pobst, Dick, and Carl Richards. *The Caddisfly Handbook: An Orvis Streamside Guide*. New York: Lyons Press, 1998.

Schwiebert, Ernest G., Jr. *Matching the Hatch*. New York: Macmillan, 1955.

Spector, George L. *Delaware River Fly Fishing Guide*. Portland, OR: Frank Amato, 2001.

Titus, Robert. *The Catskills in the Ice Age*, revised ed. Fleischmanns, NY: Purple Mountain Press, 2003.

Valla, Mike. *Tying Catskill-Style Dry Flies*. New Cumberland, PA: Headwater Books, 2009.

Van Put, Ed. *The Beaverkill: The History of a River and Its People*. New York: Lyons & Burford, 1996.

Van Put, Ed. *Trout Fishing in the Catskills*. New York: Skyhorse, 2007.

Weamer, Paul. *Fly-Fishing Guide to the Upper Delaware River*. Mechanicsburg, PA: Stackpole Books, 2007.

INDEX